Ascension Press

In Your Holy Spirit:
Shaping the Parish Through Spiritual Practice

Robert Gallagher

We have written two companion books. This is *In Your Holy Spirit: Shaping the Parish Through Spiritual Practice*, and is focused on how the parish church and its clergy can better support and foster the development of spiritual life and practices, and in so doing improve the health of the whole parish.

Michelle Heyne has written *In Your Holy Spirit: Traditional Spiritual Practices in Today's Christian Life*, which addresses the individual's spiritual practice.

To see more titles from Ascension Press, please visit www.orderoftheascension.org.

For information on congregational development, including training programs, papers, and other resources visit:

www.shapingtheparish.com

www.congregationaldevelopment.com

In Your Holy Spirit:
Shaping the Parish Through Spiritual Practice

Published 2011 by Ascension Press

Contents

Give them an inquiring and discerning heart, the courage to will and to persevere, a spirit to know and to love you, and the gift of joy and wonder in all your works.

The Book of Common Prayer

Introduction

The prayer on the facing page is the one offered after a person is baptized with water and before the sealing with oil. How is it that we are formed in such a manner? How is it that we grow to become people of discernment, courage, and perseverance? Lovers and friends of God? Open to joy? Given to awe and wonder? What are the habits of mind, heart and behavior we need to take on? What spiritual practices nurture us in that way? What can a parish church do that will contribute to that development?

We have written two companion books addressing spiritual practices. Michelle Heyne, working with input from Bob Gallagher, has written about spiritual practices from the perspective of the laity. Bob Gallagher, working with input from Michelle, has written about how the parish church and its clergy can better support and foster the development of spiritual life and practices. Both use the same map of spiritual practice.

The "map" we are offering includes five elements. At the base there are two practices: one weekly, one daily. That rhythm is common to many religious and spiritual traditions. These elements have to do with living in the habits and ways that keep us grounded in what is most real. In Anglicanism they take form as the Holy Eucharist (Mass, Communion) and the Daily Office (Divine Office, Liturgy of the Hours, Daily Prayer of the Church).

Then on that base there are two more elements standing side-by-side – Community and Reflection. Our assumption is that we are all called to be part of not just the broader human and national communities but also of particular, imperfect communities that we allow to nurture and influence us. In Anglicanism that includes the parish church. Reflection includes developing our capacity to be silent and still; to listen to our life; and to learn from our experience. Reflection is about connecting our life to the life of God.

The final element is service. We are all called to serve in ways that fit our gifts and temperament. That service may be most fruitful, for others and us, when it sits upon the base of the other four spiritual practices.

No one gets spiritual practices perfectly right. That's for at least two reasons: First, we are limited both by our amazing and persistent capacity to screw up life and by simple human frailty. Second, we change, and our world changes. What served us well ten years ago may no longer serve us.

Saints are developed in all sorts of parish churches. Five star parishes produce saints and so do two star parishes. In some parishes we can see how it happens and in others we are left amazed at God's patience and graciousness.

Some of the assumptions we begin with include these:

1. We all have a spiritual life.

2. It is a significant act of spiritual growth when we accept responsibility for our spiritual life.

3. A healthy spiritual life assumes engagement, rather than escape; an interest in the life of the world instead of spiritual sentimentality or being caught up in illusions.

4. We are seeking a spiritual practice with roots in ancient ways and useful in modern life.

5. We need a spirituality that is both solid and resilient.

6. Our spiritual life serves us best when we understand that it is to evolve over time. What serves us when we are 11 differs from when we are 18 and still again from when we are 35 or 60. A fertile evolution unfolds out of forms of spiritual life that are complex, rich, and paradoxical. They continue to grow as we increase our self-awareness, insight, and in response to changing circumstances.

7. It requires efficiency if it is to serve modern daily life.

8. It requires attention and time if it is to serve modern daily life.

6

9. Our spiritual life and discipline is to be based on an integrated system, a pattern, rather than a series of random practices. We are to live our spiritual life by Rule, not rules.

10. It is possible for the average church member to become competent and proficient in spiritual practices.

11. We must decide to base our spiritual life on persistence, courage, and competence, rather than on feelings—whether we feel like praying or not. A useful and faithful spiritual life requires critical reasoning and intelligences. We need to intentionally turn away from spiritual fads and fast food.

12. The parish church's primary task is the spiritual formation of its people.

Clearly we must work hard.

Saint Teresa of Avila

One

Shaping the Parish

These books are a resource for a parish to use with just about any regular attendee and those who have started attending on a regular basis. They can provide the base for an orientation to spiritual practice offered several times each year as part of the parish's incorporation process.

Beyond that initial offering, it's part of the priest's work to identify those ready to take more responsibility for their own spiritual life. They may be people who are ready to move from an immature or tentative faith to something more solid, or it may be people who have had a stable pattern for many years and are in need of renewal by giving more shape to their spiritual practices.

It's important that we notice when a person is ready for solid food or new ways. This time of spiritual and emotional readiness is a time of receptivity, a time when the person may be especially open to training and guidance.

In Western society today we might assume that most of those who begin to attend the Eucharist on a regular basis have made a decision to enter into the Christian life. However, they may not know enough about what that involves to be proficient.

Parishes may want to set a goal of being able to incorporate a person within five months of their first Sunday. Not every person will cooperate with that process, but many will. The parish can orient all those willing to the basics of spiritual practice. The likelihood of a stable commitment to the parish is increased if within a few months of beginning to attend a person knows how to participate and engage in the Eucharist and has a basic grasp of spiritual practices.

That orientation might include:

- Participating in a five or six session introduction to spiritual practice grounded in the church's tradition and incorporating a rule of life. An alternate possibility would be to offer it as a module in a more extensive introduction.
- Providing a Bible and Prayer Book to each person along with the companion book by Michelle Heyne on individual practice.
- Having the person do a self-assessment of spiritual practices and be in conversation with others doing the same.
- A conversation with the priest or other spiritual guide about what more the person might be seeking, if anything.

The barriers

Among the barriers to developing a healthy, vibrant parish life are the inadequate mental models[1] held by many parish leaders and expressed in parish life. Among those models are the following.

- The pattern of corporate worship is Sunday Eucharist at 8 and 10, Wednesday at 9:30 am (or possibly 5:30). Along with this goes the assumption that an Episcopal priest doesn't have the energy to celebrate the Eucharist more than twice on Sunday.
- The Daily Practice is "whatever!" Any spiritual custom you pick will do.
- The justification for the parish's existence is something about the number of programs, or outreach, new members, or that it's "a warm parish family."
- The parish community deals with inclusion by trying to reduce discomfort. Because safety is so important, tentative and superficial relationships are the norm.
- The target for growth is "young people." To reach them, the "traditionals" want a youth group and, if they have the money, a youth minister; the "progressives" want an emergent church.

The problem we face is that we carry mental models that are inadequate for our current and future needs. These are not deliberate lies told with destructive malice but partial and possibly dated truths: convincing, persistent, and naïve.

Changing our way of thinking

I am suggesting in this book that we change the mental models. That we shift to other models that express a deeper part of our common life. The change is toward grounding ourselves in our own tradition, including that part of the tradition that assumes experimentation in the spiritual life.

The pattern I believe called for in our age includes a weekly and a daily practice connecting us to something larger than ourselves; practices that link us to the ancient rhythms and bring us into relationship with the baptized community. It also includes a way to recover and maintain a sense of perspective about the world and ourselves.

Helping people enter into such change requires a shift in the thinking pattern. We know that many people approach the Christian life along lines such as, "I need to attend church on Sunday and be good person during the week." Pretty much what they picked up by age eight.

Our task is to suggest to people that they substitute that with two other lines of thought.

1. What do I need to do to stay grounded in Christ? What do I need to do to grow as a person? What will help me grow in perseverance, joy and wonder; in love, faith and hope?
2. How may I become competent in the spiritual life? What are the maps that can help me shape a balanced approach? What are the practices and skills I need?

This is a shift from "having the answer" to asking the questions. It is a shift from the assumptions of a child to those of an adult.

The decision for parishes

There is a polarity inherent in all relationships and institutions:

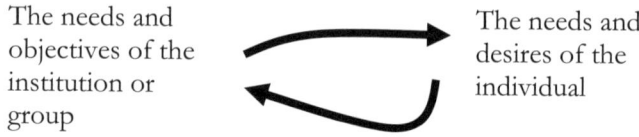

| The needs and objectives of the institution or group | | The needs and desires of the individual |

All leaders face the question of how the life of the group or institution will adequately attend to each pole. The field of organization development has the issue as one of its central concerns. The polarity is a core dynamic of every parish church.

Whether we are dealing with the most staid established parish or one of the more recent emergent church congregations, all churches live someplace between:

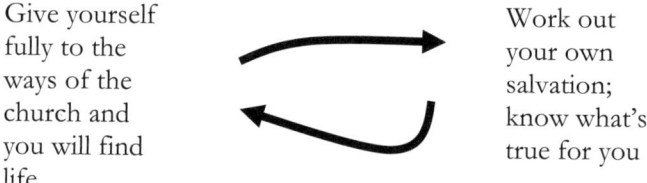

| Give yourself fully to the ways of the church and you will find life | | Work out your own salvation; know what's true for you |

On the further ends of the spectrum each can take on a tone of "we are the true church" or "this is how Jesus would do things." Most of us live someplace in between, maybe out of "it's what we're used to" and maybe out of a bit of humility.

My own experience is that it is parishes grounded in the ancient ways of the tradition, and also willing to experiment with new ways of living in the tradition, that are effectively forming Christians as well as attracting new members, both younger and older. This is also the place it will happen if there is to be a new outburst of spiritual life that touches a significant number of people.

A problem we face in many parishes is that we make two interrelated errors. We don't really equip people in the tradition of spiritual practice, and neither do we have an adequate spirit of innovation and experimentation regarding spiritual practice. Some will manage these things on their own and make use of the parish's sporadic offerings to help them do so.

Others will struggle to create something that feels both useful and adaptive. As one pastor in an evangelical emergent church suggested, "We have been making this stuff up," and noted that the Episcopal Church already has the ancient ways as part of its heritage and life.

Many Episcopal lay people know and use practices that are at the core of our tradition, but have received little support from their parish clergy or in the way parish life is lived. The lovely image of "ancient future" isn't something we have to make up. It's part of who we are. The challenge in many cases is to engage the ancient practices with the imagination and persistence needed to adapt them to our common and individual lives.

Diana Butler Bass saw the same triad in the churches in her study: "connection to tradition, commitment to Christian practices, and concern to live God's dream."[2] Intentionality about practices can produce a sense of energy and liveliness that has its own value while also making the parish more attractive to potential members.

A map of spiritual practice

I find myself coming at this with a focus on five things: weekly practice (Eucharist), daily practice (some form of the Daily Prayer of the Church), reflectiveness (some way to get perspective, to ground life), participation in the parish community, and service. I believe that's the primary baptismal tradition of the church. I am finding it helpful to simply stay focused on those five elements.

Given who I am and the way my life is, it becomes for me a matter of innovating and experimenting to make it all work. I frequently miss the Sunday Eucharist because I'm on a plane from DC to Seattle. The Wednesday mass at Trinity Parish, Seattle, is the most regular Eucharistic community I'm part of.

The daily routine has been harder for me. I have taken to posting a sign over the computer, trying to discipline myself to do it before I get into e-mail, and focusing on the three core elements of the Office. So, I get on the web, do one psalm, one reading, the collect for the day, and a few intercessions. If I do more, that's great; but I hold myself accountable for the core practice.

My reflectiveness is very connected with walking and a few people with whom I have regular lunches or after-work drinks. If I walk for more than 15 minutes I find my own inner silence. I usually start pondering and wondering.

Michelle and I usually get together each Wednesday before the 5:30 Eucharist and catch up. John and I have lunch every couple of weeks, and Bryan and Amanda and I will have an occasional dinner together. Miriam and I go through periods of intense exchange about our lives by e-mail. My work brings me back in contact with friends like Scott and Susan a few times each year, more during periods of crisis. Those meetings are also times of reflection. Friendships are a significant element of reflectiveness for me. There are also regular times with my therapist, as well as mutual spiritual guidance during the yearly retreat of Order of the Ascension.

I'm never quite satisfied with how I participate in the parish community. It's largely related to my introversion. I like one-on-one and small groups of old friends. So, that's mostly how I do it. I find a friend or two in the parish and spend time with them. On occasion I'll stretch and participate in "dinners for eight." If I'm in town for an extended period of time I might join in coffee hour. I keep thinking I should do more. I imagine that the more extraverted feel the same about reflection and silence.

That's how it works for me. This book is about how a parish church can support members in finding their own way of grounding life in the spiritual practices of the church. It's more about the renewal end of things as opposed to the apostolate.

This is about offering the tradition to our people and inviting them to appropriate it and adapt it to their lives in a process of innovation and experimentation. The tone we take is important. This isn't a "should" carrying the implication that there is something wrong with a person if they don't join in.

One of the reasons I love the Episcopal Church is that it has provided many of us space to experiment beyond the tradition, or at least to stretch things in ways that some saw as outside the tradition. The first Mass I celebrated was at a table in the West Philadelphia commune I was a member of in the early 70s. I have a special fondness for the Community of Julian of Norwich where I was vicar during the 90s. We did communal liturgical dance, incorporated jazz into the liturgy, and had shared homilies every Sunday.

The experimenting seen in some of the emerging church congregations feels familiar. That space for experimentation leads to some truly weird innovations alongside the moments of grace and wonder. There needs to be a place for experimentation in the parish church, but this book isn't about that.

This is about spaces of stability and continuity, of grounding and connection with what is truly ancient. Experimentation and innovation are in this case *servants of appropriating the tradition*, making it accessible in particular settings for a variety of personalities. This book is about most Episcopal parishes, what they are and what they can be.

The Shape of the Parish

The Shape of the Parish model[3] is a resource for understanding a parish's spiritual dynamics. It's also a strategy for moving the parish toward increased health and faithfulness. (See the Resources section for a summary of the model.)

The parish is made up of people at various stages of the journey. They have different spiritualities, some more mature than others.

There are people with a stable, disciplined, competence; they are proficient as baptized members of the Body. Others are regular in their participation in the Sunday Eucharist with some progressing toward something deeper and broader, while others have settled into a fruitful pattern, and still others who attend but may be frequently uncertain about why. There are people who show up on Christmas, Easter and special events and usually a group, some of them not known to the parish, with a vicarious connection.

At the heart of the pastoral strategy for shaping the parish is to both *accept* people where they are and also to *invite* them to move beyond where they are. In regard to the system of the parish the task is to set loose a dynamic and develop a climate that expresses and so draws people deeper into faith.

"When a parish has a healthy and productive Shape you see a definite movement. People are drawn into a deeper relationship with God and the church. There is a sense of spiritual movement in the parish."[4]

Leaders are establishing two dynamics at the center in shaping the parish. They are the deep underlying assumptions that provide the base for a healthy parish culture. The parish church is about forming people for "real life;" for maturity in Christ. It is developing in women and men a taste for life in what John Macquarrie saw as "a commonwealth of free, responsible beings united in love." Secondly, the parish is about engaging "an energy not its own."

Formation isn't about creating perfect, sinless people. It is about connecting us to the power of the Holy Spirit.[5]

The Demand System

Heavenly Father, in you we live and move and have our being: We humbly pray you so to guide and govern us by your Holy Spirit, that in all the cares and occupations of our life we may not forget you, but may remember that we are ever walking in your sight; through Jesus Christ our Lord.

A Collect for Guidance, *Book of Common Prayer*

The prayer rightly assumes that we lose track of what's most important. We get caught up in all the "cares and occupations of our life." We just do, and we will.

In organization development there is an assumption that all organizations have a "demand system." That demand system is the web of expectations and pressures calling for energy, time and money. The demands may be external or internal. All parishes have the regular flow of work they must attend to. There's the occasional crisis, problems to solve and deadlines to meet. We also get caught up in work that just isn't very important to what we exist to do and be. Some meetings, phone calls and e-mail are like that. Most of us also have routines that are in fact either busy-work or time wasters.

All those things, the important and the unimportant, consume most parishes and most of our individual lives.

The activities that transform parish and personal life can take a back seat to the routine business that must be done and to the unimportant interruptions and trivia of life. What renews life and develops the parish waits for when there's time. This means relationships don't get built, people don't receive training and coaching in spiritual practices, strategic issues aren't addressed, and so opportunities are missed and crises not foreseen and prevented.

We can turn all that around by adding elements to the demand system. We need to add activities and resources into parish life that keep the important, transformative matters in front of us. In congregational development it means things like a yearly leadership retreat that works only on strategic matters; having a skilled external consultant; leaders receiving in-depth leadership training for congregational development, and developing a richer parish life of prayer through the Daily Office and increasing the ability of members for participation in the Eucharist and their own personal devotions.

In relationship to spiritual practices it may mean taking actions such as:

- Scheduling Evening Prayer Monday through Friday and recruiting teams of two or more people to cover each evening.

- Parish clergy changing their schedule so they can be at Evening Prayer most days.

- Creating and scheduling a Foundations Course, with at least three units of three sessions each per year.

- Otherwise aligning the practices of the parish and of the clergy with behavior consistent with its priorities.

As Stephen Covey said, "The key is not to prioritize what's on your schedule, but to schedule your priorities."

A system of spiritual practice

This book offers a map of spiritual practice grounded in Anglican spirituality. That map is a system of spiritual life rather than a list of assorted practices. A useful system will provide a balance of nurture and stretching. It will include our inner life and our outer life. It will draw on what is ancient in the service of today and the future.

In such a system our inclinations and gifts are supported and allowed to flourish and the less developed parts of us are drawn out and developed. All so we may become stronger in love and faith, more resilient, with a broader mind and an enlarged heart. So, we may live in the embrace of the Glorious Trinity.

Maps are useful things.

1. They are based on the experience of others. This is how many others have made the journey.

2. They help you get somewhere. If you want to grow in the spiritual life it may help to have a guide.

3. They change as the circumstances of life change. In a world of rapid change and loose ties among people we have an increased need for a sense of perspective, being in community, and engaging daily routines that give us ground to stand upon.

4. They are only useful if people find them useful. People vary in temperament and spiritual inclination. Maps can provide too much or too little detail for different groups of people. The old maps, whether of 1900 or of 1976, continue to serve those able to embrace them. Our hope is that the map we offer here will serve many people seeking ancient practices to help them effectively and faithfully engage contemporary life.

William James said that religious belief is "the belief that there is an unseen order, and that our supreme good lies in harmoniously adjusting ourselves thereto." James was speaking of much more than something like a spiritual map. His concern may have been more akin to the writer of Hebrews, "faith is the assurance of things hoped for, the conviction of things not seen." But at the boundaries of that unseen order exist all the practices that bring us into unity, give us hope and faith, and help us abide in love. These are the ancient ways of the spiritual life that maps of spiritual practice make more visible and accessible.

The primary task

The primary job of church is to be a spiritual community that forms people in faith. Diana Butler Bass, *Christianity for the Rest of Us*, Harper One, 2006, p. 42

The primary task[6] of an organization is the most central and fundamental process used in fulfilling its mission. Awareness of the primary task allows us to devote our resources in the service of what's most essential. If we can pull together significant resources in support of the primary task we may be more effective as a parish. We are placing our human, material and financial resources toward what we exist to be and do.

The primary thing a parish church does toward fulfilling the church's mission is to form people in Christ. In *Fill All Things* I suggested a framework for thinking about it. The Renewal – Apostolate Cycle (see Resource section) describes the Christian's movement between being renewed in baptismal identity and

19

purpose and living as instruments of God's love and grace in daily life. The Cycle is interested in both the individual's movement and in the ways in which the parish church supports and facilitates that movement.

To quote Stephen Covey again, "The main thing is to keep the main thing the main thing." Equipping people in the core spiritual practices is part of what the parish does to keep the main thing the main thing.

Shaping the Parish

Grounding → Integration → Action

1. Parish clergy can set a goal in their own mind of within the next three years:

   a) Stabilizing their own spiritual practice

   b) Having 15 - 20% of the adult average Sunday attendance engaged in "apostolic faith" practice

   c) 80% of the adult average Sunday attendance aware of the core spiritual practices and 30% proficient.

2. If members are on the whole unformed in spiritual practices develop a pastoral – spiritual life strategy to arrive at the above goals. Look for ways to introduce spiritual practices in training programs, written material, sermons, and spiritual guidance.

3. Provide either an adequate overall orientation to spiritual practices within the first five months of a person's arrival in the parish and/or a module of a more complete training program (See the Resources section for an outline of such a program – "Anglican Spirituality"). Make it a priority to ground new members in spiritual practice. You might offer a three session orientation several times each year regardless of the size of the parish or you might have a more extensive program of five modules, one on each

20

element of the map, three session each, conducted over a two year period, and then repeated.

Eucharist & Office

The peculiarity of the Anglican tradition is the equal emphasis which it gives to the Divine Office and the Eucharist; that is to say, to Biblical and to Sacramental worship. Where this balance is disturbed, its special character is lost. ...It is, I believe, by the balanced and instructed development of these two great instruments of Christian worship—carrying them forward without deflection from their supernatural orientation, yet keeping them flexible to the changing spiritual needs and spiritual insights of the world—that the Anglican Communion will best fulfill its liturgical office within the Body of Christ. Here support and stimulus is given to the Godward life of the individual, while the solemn objectivity of true Catholic worship is preserved.

-Evelyn Underhill, *Worship* 1936, pp.335-336

"Underhill refers to the pattern we see in *The Book of Common Prayer*. About two-thirds of the book is taken up with the Eucharist, the Office, and materials to support those acts of worship (lectionaries, the Psalms). *The Book of Common Prayer* isn't a book of personal devotions, but its spirituality does assume that the Christian will find ways of personal devotion that are appropriate to their own personality and growth in love."[7]

There's a leaflet that was put out by the Diocese of Texas at one point that confused the nature of daily prayer. It included in the Q & A section the question, "Can I make up my own prayers?" The answer was, *"The Book of Common Prayer* is meant to complement daily individual prayers, not to replace them."

An answer more grounded in our understanding of Anglican spirituality might have been, "People can always pray on their own and phrase those prayers as they want. The assumption of the Church, however, is that the Sunday Eucharist and the Daily Prayer

21

of the Church (Daily Office) shape our minds and hearts so our individual reflections and prayers are grounded in the broader and more ancient ways of God's church. Our common prayer, done as corporate worship or as individuals, is the foundation orienting us to a right relationship with God, one another, self and creation."

A shorter version might say, "The Eucharist and Daily Office are the ground on which our personal reflection and devotions are built. The common prayer of the church is a gift that can shape our hearts and minds, can root us in true religion and deep spirituality." In other words, our individual prayers are to complement the common prayer of the Church in Eucharist and Office.

The Texas leaflet also contained another misunderstanding about spiritual practice. It assumed that "common prayer" meant corporate worship, worship done together, when in fact it is "common prayer" when ten people say a form of Morning Prayer even though not in the same place at the same time. It is "common" because it is the *church's* daily prayer, whether said in community or as individuals.

Reflection & Community

Reflection and community are related needs in the spiritual life. Reflection, which is always grounded in our capacity for inner silence, is our pathway to God dwelling in us. We are made for community, wired for connection with others. We long to be accepted, treasured and trusted by others.

In our world the primary places that can help us integrate life are in developing a capacity for reflection and being part of a community that we allow to nurture and influence us.

There are moments

We have all experienced moments when we see more clearly and experience things more fully. Times when we seem to be more open to adoration and awe, joy and wonder. Times of a rich interior life. Moments of harmony and unity with ourselves, others, the creation and God.

These times come as a gift that is suddenly present during the Eucharist or an Office, in our reflections, when with others in community, or as we serve. It's as though the inner life of things is finding expression; things unseen are for a moment seen. We don't control all this. We can however place ourselves in the pathways of grace. We can give ourselves to the ancient ways and the spiritual rhythms others have used before us. In those acts of humility we may also find more occasions of harmony and growth.

The measure

The measure is Christ. We are all subconsciously inclined to define spiritual and emotional maturity in terms of where we are now. We limit ourselves to the "is" of the current moment.

It helps to say to ourselves, "There's more, more to life, more to me; my life is hid with Christ in God." I find it helpful to look to the saints and the Christians I know who live a proficient spiritual life. Looking to them gives me hope and invites me to continue on the way.

There's a psychological trick we can use to avoid the challenge we experience in looking to the Christ, the saints and martyrs, and the apostolic faithful. On the one hand we can find fault with them, find their feet of clay. On the other hand we can raise them above us and find comfort in thinking we could never be like them. All of that needs to be set aside. In the end we are all called into the likeness of God, the maturity of Christ. In the meantime, in life and in death, we are called to live the prayer of "continual growth in thy love and service; and ... to follow the good examples of all thy saints."

That which we have heard and known

Episcopalians pass on "the mysteries of ancient times"[8] through a life of prayer, reflection, life in community and service to others.

Shaping the Parish™: The Program

Shaping the Parish™ is a program to equip lay and ordained leaders to develop and nurture healthier parishes. It focuses on immediate, tangible improvements while building long-term health. Shaping the Parish™ assumes that vibrant, faithful churches will flourish as leaders and parishes improve their own: spiritual practice, emotional and social intelligence, change theory and methods. For more information see www.shapingtheparish.com.

A Map: Spiritual Practices

Service

↑   ↑   ↑   ↑   ↑

Reflection Community

↑   ↑   ↑   ↑   ↑

Eucharist Daily Prayers
of the Church

TRINITY

Life in the community of the Trinity

A state of being entered into at baptism. God:
beyond us, beside us, within us.

*The unifying of the personality, the integration of mind
and heart into one center* (Leech)

My life shall be a real life, being wholly full of Thee.
(St. Augustine)

*The end ... would be a commonwealth of free,
responsible beings united in love* (John Macquarrie)

A map of spiritual practice for the parish might look something like this:

Weekly Practice: Holy Eucharist

The Holy Eucharist celebrated several times each week as to allow people with a variety of schedules to find one that might serve as their weekly spiritual practice.

Daily Practice: The Daily Prayers of the Church

There are two things to do here. The first is to equip and support parishioners in saying the Daily Prayer of the Church on their own in the course of daily life. The second is to offer the Daily Office in some routine form on most days of the week.

Reflection

There are two primary acts for the parish to take. One is to offer members assistance in identifying and maintaining ways of being reflective. The second is for the parish itself to engage in reflective processes, ways of listening to and learning from its own life as a community. The beginning place for this is to create an environment with significant space for stillness and silence.

Parish Community

The parish needs to provide opportunities for social life among parishioners and create an environment in which they may find and live what Augustine called a "real life," a life in which they might be genuine, be open and honest about themselves, and still be in deep relationship with others and God. This is a community where our differences can be expressed and will be accepted; in which we can fight with those we love without fearing the loss of the relationship.

Serve

The parish can hold in front of its members the moral vision of Christian Faith. The primary place, the most effective place, of service for the Christian is in his or her daily life. We serve within our friendships, families, work, and civic life. The parish can help members identify how they serve, how they may better serve, and the gifts each brings to that task. The parish can also have at least one service ministry that is done as a parish. This is a call to a wise and generous love.

The Process of Change

The parish can provide a foundations program that equips people to take responsibility for their own spiritual life and moral action in daily life. It can also model an approach to change or experimentation and learning from experience. It can teach methods that allow people to face change.

For the fully Christian life is a Eucharistic life: that is, a natural life conformed to the pattern of Jesus, given in its wholeness to God, laid on His altar as a sacrifice of love, and consecrated, transformed by His inpouring life, to be used to give life and food to other souls.

Evelyn Underhill

Two
The Weekly Practice: Holy Eucharist

The Holy Eucharist is the weekly spiritual practice for Episcopalians and indeed for most Christians. For almost all of us it's a Sunday morning practice; for some it's engaged at other times during the week. For the past few years I've traveled a good bit on Sunday morning and have found myself thinking of the Wednesday 5:30 p.m. Eucharist at Trinity, Seattle as my weekly practice.

The Eucharist, along with the Daily Office, is both the ground and the completion of spiritual practice. These liturgical acts unify the person in the Body of Christ; they allow us to express the purpose for which we exist, to glorify, love and serve God. Our reflection, life in community, and service are dependent on Eucharist and the Daily Prayers of the Church. In the Eucharist people are evangelized and formed in Christ.

So, liturgy is about worship. It is not about us being comfortable, not about us learning something. It is an opportunity for wonder and awe, an opportunity to offer ourselves to God and be "in" God. We lose that opportunity when we focus on comfort or learning. Of course, it's also a fine thing if along the way we learn something or become familiar with and comfortable with the Eucharist.

The Eucharist is now such a central part of parish life it is like the air we breathe. There's nothing much to say about it—we assume it. In many ways that's as it should be.

The Eucharist sums up in itself Christian worship...It seems to include everything. It combines Word and Sacrament; its appeal is to spirit and to sense...; it is communion with God and communion with man..... Gathers up in itself the meaning of the church; its whole action implies and sets forth our mutual interdependence in the Body of Christ; it unites us with

29

the Church of the past ...; an anticipation of the heavenly banquet.
John MacQuarrie, *Paths in Spirituality*

Do it well

The primary thing a parish can do in regard to the Eucharist and the spiritual life of members is to do it well.

Following are some of the elements we might consider in trying to do it well. They apply to those presiding, those serving, and those in the congregation, as well as the liturgical space itself.

For example, you are seeking a liturgical space that is graceful, uncluttered and beautiful, one that fits the congregation's size and style of worship. The space needs to allow those serving at the altar and in the congregation to move about without awkwardness. It needs to manage the polarity of expressing stability, that this is "sacred space," along with allowing for a degree of flexibility. It needs to work for a variety of uses—Sunday morning Eucharist, a small group gathered for the Daily Office, a Wednesday centering prayer group, and possibly performances of music or drama.

Elements of "doing it well"

Climate

Seek an overall climate or tone of apostolic faith. Orient things toward the participation of the spiritually mature rather than those of a more tentative faith. The feeling should be like the heavenly banquet, a taste of Glory for those who are competent in the ways of the liturgy and the church's spirituality. Find ways to create beauty, reverence, the experience of a grounded, calm community rather than of busyness and rush. Solemn[9] but not fussy. While oriented toward the apostolic there needs to be space for those who are more tentative and unformed. That's partly done by humility and humor in sermons and at coffee hour.

The climate is strongly influenced by an appropriate liturgical presence[10] of those serving at the altar. We can learn to live in the

30

paradox of seeking to do things perfectly while not getting agitated about mistakes, of being confident and self–aware without being arrogant or fastidious. A rushed and anxious environment before the beginning of the Eucharist can undercut an appropriate climate.

Competence

Give the time and energy needed to equip those with a special role in the celebration, e.g., cantor, lector, ministers of the altar, acolyte. There's something unkind about leaving people to wander around the altar looking and feeling confused because of inadequate training and coaching.

The presiding clergy should demonstrate awareness of their impact during the liturgy. Eccentric and clueless behavior, excessive control, being unprepared, are all uncommon. Clergy generally understand the principles of good liturgy but may not be clear when their own behavior has an unintended negative impact on worship. Parishes should put in place ways to provide feedback to the clergy on their liturgical presence.

The most important competency is that of the congregation. Some parishes emphasize "hospitality" and "being welcoming" at the expense of good liturgy. There is, though, a form of hospitality that doesn't destroy the liturgy or connection among members with excessive concerns about "comfort" and "user friendliness." Paying attention to building competence allows newcomers to experience the grace and dignity of worship while becoming more skilled in their own participation. It may help to remember that we are managing polarities here (being welcoming AND doing liturgy well), not trading off one value for another.

Pattern

Shortly before I began my duties as vicar of St. Elisabeth's, I asked people what they thought about the liturgy. The first and unanimous response was, "Can it be the same for a few weeks in a row?" The congregation had been unable to develop a sense of "common prayer" because the priest thought they needed to be exposed to more interesting variations. Apparently they had been experiencing enough changes from one week to the next that they

31

were not able to develop the needed ownership of the liturgy. They felt incompetent.

Some of the most common mistakes made are:

- Rotating between or among rites weekly.

- Rotating elements of the liturgy frequently, such as the mass settings used or the Great Thanksgiving.

Less common are:

- Trapping people in a parish meeting by not doing the blessing until the meeting is over.

- Disconnecting the offering of money from the offering of bread and wine.

- Having the sermon after the Eucharist.

Liturgy has a shape. Liturgy is a movement from one place to another. Our understanding of and conformity with that shape and direction allows people to participate. It also offers a deeper, more rewarding experience.

Flow

This is about allowing people to have the experience of being immersed in the liturgical event. It involves an opportunity for depth and focus, of an involvement in which there is a lack of self-consciousness, and a sense of personal ownership provided because the person has the competencies needed to fully engage the experience. The person is carried along as in the current of a stream.

Flow is enabled by stability in liturgical practices, the climate established by the space and liturgical ministers, and intentionally developing the competency of the congregation.

Congruence

Liturgy is an activity that calls for aesthetical harmony. There's a reliable relationship of elements. It assists the person in having a sense of oneness with self, others, and God. An example of lack of congruence has emerged in some parishes that print the entire liturgy for the day in a leaflet. During the Gospel procession and reading many people have their noses in the leaflet, following along instead of looking at the reader. The procession and deacon's reading of the Gospel finds itself in competition with the leaflet. When parishes see the incongruity they stop printing that reading in the leaflet. That can lead them to see the same difficulty with printing the other readings and the Great Thanksgiving. The fullest sense of participation for people comes with an awareness of the liturgical action, others in the congregation, and the sacred space.

Proportion

Proportion is about the liturgy and the space. The relationship among elements seems in accord, in balance. The sermon or the music doesn't have the effect of overwhelming the rest. The altar, font, and lectern fit one another and the scale of the total space. The ceremony works with the space.

Appropriateness

What is done fits the setting, occasion, and people gathered. Common mistakes around appropriateness include inviting an excessive degree of interpersonal intimacy, tilting too much toward extraversion or introversion, and forcing physical activity that a significant number of people find difficult. The competencies required for good liturgy, for flow and climate, are necessary objectives that need to be accomplished without creating a counter productive clumsiness and discomfort among people.

Acceptance & Accessibility

To manage this properly requires practical judgment and a sense of proportion. For example, you don't change over to all gluten-free wafers because some have that need, or make a Eucharist so child-friendly that it becomes unsatisfying or embarrassing for most adults who participate. We don't change the elements of bread and wine because there are alcoholics in the parish. We maintain the ancient practice of incense even though a few have allergies.

There are other values in liturgy besides inclusivity. Similarly, acceptance is a two-way street. People are welcomed in and invited to take on the ways of the community. I can take my allergy pill so we can all enjoy the sight and smell of incense. I can receive in one kind so most can receive the bread and wine.

What we are to do is build ramps and spend the money to have them be both functional and attractive. We are to seek out hypoallergenic incense. There are of course limits faced by most parishes. There are people who suffer from agoraphobia and find it impossible to participate in corporate worship at the parish church. Less extreme situations might be deafness or children with extreme behavior issues. No parish will be able to be fully inclusive of every single person with all the range of difficulties and conditions, but much can be done to accommodate a variety of needs in a region or diocese.

These issues may bring out a callous attitude on the part of some and an insistent assertion of "rights" by others. It does seem to provide an opportunity for learning to live in community and mature as a person—"through love, be servants of one another" (Galatians 5:13); "with all humility and gentleness, with patience, bearing with one another in love," (Ephesians 4:2); "be subject to one another out of reverence for Christ" (Ephesians. 5:21).

As in all of parish life, it is important to tilt in the direction of apostolic faith and emotional maturity in how people participate in the Eucharist. Some key elements of that tilt include:

- Make the Eucharist an experience of grace and beauty that in its ordinary expression draws people to God and their own deepest self. "Doing it well."

- Permission to just "be." Give visitors permission to not participate. Tell people that it's fine to rest and allow the congregation to carry them in its prayer. St. Paul's Church in D.C., a parish known for its formal, Anglo-Catholic style of worship, has a statement at the beginning of the Sunday bulletin that says in part, "Welcome! We are glad you are worshiping with us today. We invite you to participate in our service, or simply observe, as you wish. If you are not familiar with our customs, your neighbors will be happy to help or explain."

- Competence. Allow the congregation to act as though it is a community participating in its primary activity rather than as an audience being guided through an unfamiliar exercise. Avoid directions about page numbers and posture, and ushers that control the people's procession to communion. Let the Liturgy speak for itself. Some parishes now have a tendency to interfere with the power and beauty of the Eucharist by introducing, explaining, and over-controlling.

Building competency – increasing Christian proficiency

The parish can offer resources that will facilitate people's mature and competent participation.

Orientation sessions[11]

This is a session of about one hour in which there is an experiential walk-through. "Experiential" means that people do something, experience it, and then have a structured opportunity to reflect on that experience.

In this session, people are invited to try things—solemn bows or genuflecting when entering the row of pews or seats, bowing as the cross passes in procession, crossing oneself at various points in the liturgy, actively listening to the sermon, an imaginative engagement during the offertory and so on.

The participants aren't told they must do things in a certain way or that they must do them going forward. Rather this is about expanding their range of choice and behavior. They are asked to try some practice from the tradition—even if they never do it again, they are asked to try it this once to see what it's like. Along the way time is provided for people to reflect on what they are experiencing, how it feels, what thoughts or feelings it sets off in them. *This is not the traditional instructed Eucharist.* It is experiential learning—do it, reflect on it, try it again.

These orientation sessions might best be done after the primary Sunday Eucharist. Allow a few minutes at coffee hour and then invite everyone interested to gather in the liturgical space. Provide a handout that contains the text of the Eucharist with notes identifying the elements that will be explored in the session. The orientation session needs to be offered several times each year.

A longer-term goal is to build a critical mass of people who know how to participate in the Liturgy. A second, shorter-term goal is to help new members become more at ease in celebrating the Eucharist. The exact number of times it's offered will depend on the number of new people attending. Most parishes will want at least three per year. The sessions work fine, even with just a few participants.

A friend, Meg Wakeman, wrote about her experience of such an orientation. "I became aware after taking the class that the more physical aspects of worship (crossing myself, genuflecting, even following the service without reading along) create a more kinesthetic connection from my body to my soul. It is not an emotional connection. This is a deeper understanding on a physical level from doing those actions and knowing what they mean. And doing them in community just makes the connection stronger. There have been times during the service where I feel as though there's a string literally tugging my heart and gently pulling it to something I don't yet understand, but that is good."

Written material

Parishes can provide booklets orienting people to Eucharistic practices. It helps to have a large stack of the booklets at several locations.[12]

Adult foundations course - session on the Eucharist

This is an expanded version of the orientation session idea. Within the parish's adult foundations course could be the same one-hour orientation that is enhanced with additional work to assist people as they participate in the Eucharist and lead a Eucharistic life.

What shall we invite them to do?

There are three primary ways people join in the Holy Eucharist: Be Present, Participate, and Engage.

Be present

People need to be told that it matters that they are just present. There are the community-oriented reasons having to do with enjoying each other's companionship in the Liturgy, loving one another, and missing people when they are absent. At a more profound level there's this: the worship of God in the Eucharist is the reason we exist. We exist to participate in the life and glory of God and it is in the Eucharist that life is focused and actualized.

In the Liturgy, we the baptized participate in the worship of God in union with Christ, the church throughout the world, and with "angels and archangels and the whole company of heaven."

Just be present. Follow along as well as you are able that day. Let go of all the judgments about how you may not being paying enough attention or how you're not feeling especially pious. To accept that the essential act is being there is the practice of humility. It is also a statement that you have grown up enough to realize that it is foolish to allow your passing feelings to control your spiritual life. Because we give ourselves by being present, on occasion we receive the gift of being touched by deep joy, awe, and a sense of the harmony that exists within all things.

We begin with obedience and humility, not passion and devotion. The Eucharist is first an act of God and of the Body of Christ of which you and I are members. We can make a choice to set ourselves in the places of grace, in the holy spaces in which God has promised to be with us.

Participate

The parish can do a great deal to assist people in becoming competent participants in the Eucharist. The starting place is simple. Parishioners can learn the sequence and the common responses. They can be encouraged to develop the habit of setting the book aside and allowing their attention to be on the liturgical action—looking at the reader not the readings in a leaflet; during the Great Thanksgiving striving to be aware of the community they are with and the actions at the altar.

Our tradition makes much use of the body in liturgy. We stand, kneel, and sit; some cross themselves, bow and genuflect. We see, smell, hear, touch, and taste. When offering choices about participating, don't start by explaining the meaning of actions. Instead let it be more experiential. Have people try things on. Do it and then reflect on it.

Here are a few examples of practices that connect people to sound Eucharistic practice. Ask people to:

- Look toward the liturgical action. Look at the reader of the readings and the Gospel; look at the actions at the altar during the Great Thanksgiving, rather than down at a printed sheet. The parish can facilitate that by not printing the readings and the text of the Great Thanksgiving in a bulletin. An awareness of the liturgical action both expresses and fosters the unity of the church.

- Move forward at the "Invitation." When the celebrant says "The Gifts of God for the People of God" the congregation is to move toward the places where communion is distributed. It is the people's procession to communion. There should be none of the Victorian nonsense of ushers guiding or controlling this movement. As the ministers of the altar are receiving communion the whole congregation needs to be gathering so it may also receive.[13]

- Receive both bread and wine, including receiving from the common cup.[14]

Engage

The particulars will vary from person to person, temperament to temperament. Because the purpose of the Eucharist is to worship God in union with the whole church and Christ the head of the church, these forms of engagement are secondary to simply being present and participating.

Here are a few methods of engagement that can be taught.

- Intercession during the Eucharist. One tradition is to have a special intention in mind. Carry someone or a concern on your heart before God. If you think of it at the time, offer it during the Offertory, as though you were laying it upon the altar, pouring it into the chalice.

- Review the readings of the day before the Eucharist begins. That may be on arrival but could also be days in advance. Using a form of meditative reading may add to the experience. Focus on one of the readings. Find a phrase or word that touches you.

- Take a receptive stance during the sermon. Assume that God has a word for you. Set aside for the moment judgments about how well the preacher is doing.

- Make use of a type of affective meditative engagement. Seek a stance within yourself that fits with the part of the Eucharist happening at any given time. Maybe humility and faith during the readings and sermon; self-offering during the Offertory; unity with the whole church and with "Angels and Archangels and with all the company of heaven;" adoration during the Great Thanksgiving; communion and harmony at communion.

I recall sitting with Pat, my high school girlfriend, at a Mass in her Roman Catholic parish. Throughout the church new liturgical practices were taking hold based on a truer understanding of Liturgy. At one point in the Mass the priest stopped what he was doing, looked at the congregation, and said "please put down the rosary beads." The priest wasn't against saying the rosary but he understood that saying it during Mass was, for most people, interfering with their participation in the Eucharist.

Finding a way of engaging the Eucharist may be useful for many of us but is in no way essential. In fact there's a danger that if we are inclined to become anxious about it personal engagement will separate us from the primary activity of participating in offering this thanksgiving to God.

Seven whole days not one in seven I will praise thee; e'en eternity's too short to extol thee.

George Herbert

Three
The Daily Practice:
The Prayers of the Church

The Daily Office is the daily spiritual practice for Episcopalians.[15]

About the Office

These daily prayers of the church are a means of focusing our daily relationship with God. In this act of praise we recall and praise the Holy One and connect our prayer with the whole company of heaven. We ground ourselves in God.

The Office is daily, which is to say it's more like your daily multi-vitamin or glass of wine than the occasional steak. It's not a sin or a tragedy to forget or forgo your vitamin on some days but over time it may do you damage. In our individualism we may forget that in doing ourselves damage, we damage the whole Body.

I've recently gone through a period of several weeks when I've forgotten both the Office and my vitamin. Maybe I'll remember tomorrow. I hope so.

One of the lovely and healing things about the Office is that we can say it regardless of how we feel. We can offer it even when we don't believe.

Emily Wharton: *God has gone away* ...

Adam Dalgliesh: *My father was a parish priest. When I lost my faith he said, "If you find you can no longer believe just act as if you still do. If you feel you can no longer pray just go on saying the words."*

P.D James, *A Taste for Death*

I am convinced that the primary way modern people will use the Office is as an act of individual practice. We unite our offering with millions of Christians throughout the world who sit at kitchen tables, before computer screens, and sing it in the shower, as well as those who gather in-choir in parish churches.

Robert Benson describes how he and some friends gave shape to "praying alone together." "We promised to say the office on behalf of one another each day in case one of us was not able to pray that day. ... Every day that I fail to say my prayers, and every day that I am tempted to set the whole practice aside, I think of these people I know ... of the promises we made to one another ... to remain faithful in my prayers."[16] A member of the parish I attend once referred to the Office as "the daily prayers of the people." The Office connected her to the people of God throughout the world and through the ages.

The Office has three primary elements:

1) Psalms
2) Scripture reading
3) The church's prayers.

Around that core may be arranged introductory material, canticles, a hymn, and the creed. The psalms and reading are appointed. The prayers are those of the Church. They come from some authority outside ourselves and may therefore assist us in participating in a larger reality. This in turn may prepare us for reflection and life in community.

This is the church's prayer, not our personal devotions. It's understandable that when praying the Office alone some turn the plural pronouns (we, our) to the singular (I, my). It feels more personal. It's also a serious mistake and misses the point of the Office. Even when said alone the Office is corporate prayer. It is the church's daily prayer offered as part of the church and in union with those throughout the world who join that day in the praise of God.

So, we say "we" because we pray on behalf of, and in communion with, the whole church. It's an act of solidarity with sisters and brothers throughout the world.

Paul wrote, "Pray without ceasing." The Office was the early church's approach to respond to Paul's invitation in his first letter to the Thessalonians. It is what we mean in the baptismal covenant when we promise to "Continue ... in the prayers."

In *The Divine Hours* Phyllis Tickle offers the image of "relay runners passing a lighted torch" in writing about people who say the Office. (They) "frequently find themselves filled with a conscious awareness that they are handing their worship, at its final 'Amen,' on to other Christians in the next time zone. ... To participate in such a regimen with such an awareness is to pray, as did the Desert Fathers, from within the spiritual community of shared texts as well as within the company of innumerable other Christians, unseen but present, who have preceded one across time or who in time, will follow one."

In Tickle's forward to Robert Benson's *In Constant Prayer* she wrote, "Almost Four decades ago, the late Robert Webber gave contemporary Christians two of the greatest summarizing phrases of our faith in these postmodern, post-Christendom times. He said more and more of us were becoming 'evangelicals on the Canterbury trail' and that what we were pursuing was – and is – intimate contact with the 'ancient future.' She goes on to note that the first of the ancient disciplines to be engaged by many was the divine office."

Kenneth Leech sees the value of the Office to be its objectivity. It connects us across space and time. It provides for and encourages spiritual discipline and maturity. [17]

Nonetheless, every so often it seems especially personal. In the course of writing this I was diagnosed with cancer. A close friend wrote in response to the news a message that began with "S _ _ _" and ended with "F _ _ _."

My answer was:

I knew you'd understand. Your message has more cussing than the others. My own response seems to have two

45

primary elements - 1) s _ _ _ and f _ _ _!!! and 2) yesterday's Office, especially psalm 137 when the exiles are being asked to sing the Lord's song in upon an alien soil (I feel like I've gone into "cancer land") and 1 Peter 4: *The end of all things is near; therefore be serious and discipline yourselves for the sake of your prayers. Above all, maintain constant love for one another, ... Therefore, let those suffering in accordance with God's will entrust themselves to a faithful Creator, while continuing to do good.* I really do need to watch out here. It's not always easy to sort out self pity and sentimentality from God's word."

I had this sense that I was in a place that seemed very foreign. And I knew that if I forgot Jerusalem I'd be lost, but if I held on, I could weep and also know joy.

For me, saying the Office has been part of that slow simmering sanctification of the Spirit. Saying it whether I felt like it or not, whether it "spoke" to me or not. Trusting that this was a way of entrusting myself to "a faithful Creator." But on just a few occasions it became intensely personal. I realize that much of that has to do with what I brought to the Office that day, and that's also exactly the point.

Individual use

Begin with the individual. For the parish to effectively engage the daily practice, our spiritual guidance, preaching and educational programs need to focus on the use of the Office by individuals. We can offer training, coaching and guidance for those wanting to do the Office.

The parish can support people in using the Daily Office by:

- Showing people several web sites on the Daily Office. Have the parish web site link to the Daily Office on the web.

- Producing short forms lifted from elements of the Office in the Prayer Book

- Making it easy for members to purchase a copy of the

Book of Common Prayer (BCP) or the *Daily Office Book* from Church Publishing (includes the Four Offices, all the readings and psalms). Offer inexpensive copies of the pew type and take orders for higher quality copies. Do the same with the Bible. Offer options from among the translations approved for use in the Episcopal Church.

- Integrating training and coaching on individual use in a variety of programs.

- Supporting individual use by parish communal use.

Parish communal use

Do the Office as part of the parish's daily practice. Do it at least four days per week. Make it accessible: offer it at a time people would be most likely to participate (which in most places will be between 5:00 and 6:00 p.m.); always offer it at the same time each day; consider using a simplified format wrapped around the essential elements of psalm, reading, and the prayers; pay attention to beauty and rhythm.

How might even small and middle-sized parishes offer the Daily Prayers of the Church?

Make it easy

Select a time of the day convenient for people to attend. In most parishes that will between 5:00 and 6:00 p.m. A business district parish might find that offering Noonday Prayers that making use of one of the appointed psalms and readings will work.

Create officiant teams

Invite people to join an officiant team that is responsible for one day each week. The teams may range from two to four people. Ask people to sign up on the assumption that the whole team is present on that day. It makes it a more pleasurable activity and generates energy.

Connect

On occasion invite people to have coffee in the parish kitchen after Morning Prayer or go out for a drink together after Evening Prayer.

Orient it towards the whole parish community

In some places the Office becomes the plaything, the turf, of the individual officiant. His or her taste shapes the Office. That will distort the "common" nature of the Office and make it more difficult for others to participate. Make the flow and rhythm of the Office much the same day by day. Provide a customary, training and coaching to those willing to officiate; this shows that it is valued and worth doing well. Make it the same time every day.

Daily

Do it only if you can sustain it at least four days each week. It needs to be "daily" enough to be the daily practice. Don't turn it into an occasional service that may undermine the role of the Office in people's spiritual life, e.g., Evening Prayer only on Wednesday. If you can't manage this then focus your attention on individual use of the Office.

Be cautious, though, about making an initial assumption that it simply won't work to offer it daily at the parish. The methods described above, coupled with general formation work around Anglican spirituality and the traditional pattern of prayer and worship, can unleash significant energy in the parish.

Work with, and teach, the prayer book pattern

Sunday Eucharist, daily office (or almost daily), and personal devotions according to gift and inclination. Offer this as part of what makes for a balanced spiritual diet. Avoid things that will confuse people about the pattern (e.g., using Morning or Evening Prayer once a week, having a daily Eucharist but no Daily Office, using forms of personal devotions as corporate prayer in place of the Office.)

Clergy need to participate

Parish clergy, even those with very part-time positions, need to participate frequently. That may require adjusting other routines with family or friends. As a general rule, saying that something is important will not have impact unless the clergy also demonstrate its importance by paying attention to it and being involved. This idea is also important for scheduling of parish activities—in most cases, the parish should not schedule meetings or events during scheduled worship times.

If the parish is not going to have communal expressions of the Office it's appropriate to have a statement on the web site section on worship that reads something like this, "St. Mary's Church participates in the offering of the church's daily prayer as its members pray the Daily Office at home and workplace. This pattern of reading the appointed psalms and scripture, and saying the prayers, grounds us all in the life of God and connects us to the prayer of the whole church, living and dead."

Experiment and innovate

For the Office to become part of the parish's practice often requires a good bit of experimenting and innovation. We need to be willing to try things, reflect on the experience and draw our learnings. In several parishes I discovered that more people were ready to participate if the Office had a balance that was slightly different from what's in the Prayer Book. This involved having one reading and canticle, limiting the number of collects offered by the officiant while including a bit more silence, and a second reading from a book on the spiritual life.

Not too many years ago writers on spiritual life were wondering if the Office needed to be greatly simplified. Maybe the norm needed to be along the lines of the Daily Devotions provided at the end of the Daily Office section of the American Prayer Book. The basic structure of the Office would be maintained but the expectation of using the lectionary to find the psalm and readings would be dropped. The modern temperament just wasn't going to put up with spending all that time figuring out the details.

Since then a number of things have happened that changed the picture. The Internet made it easy to find the appointed psalm and readings, and we can now say the entire Office on line. The *Prayer Book Office* and similar resources were produced that contain all the needed material in the same book. And finally, the culture began to shift. More people were open to spending time taking on and maintaining spiritual practices.

Bishops

Many diocesan offices say the Office together each morning or join in the cathedral's offering. While it helps that the example is set, its value is in the life of the bishop and the diocesan staff.

Bishops can encourage clergy and parishes to say the Office, as well as provide broad guidelines, and a parish-based educational design for use in training officiants. See below for additional information.

Ways of undercutting Daily Practice

- Making the Office difficult to participate in by using books other than *The Book of Common Prayer*; not having a customary that all officiants use; insisting on using all the possible elements, or not doing at the same time each day.

- Making the Office so simple that its beauty and rhythm are destroyed. For example, not lighting candles, the officiant not wearing a cassock, not teaching people how to say the psalms with a pause at the asterisk.

- The clergy not participating.

- Using the Office as an occasional service rather than as daily practice. For example, just doing the Office on one evening of the week.

- The diocese requiring officiants to be licensed and to complete a course of diocesan training as a worship leader. The training needed for daily practice in the parish is: attendance and observing, a walk through, feedback and coaching. That is best done at the parish level. Diocesan training for worship leaders needs to be reserved for those likely to be officiating at large services or when Morning Prayer is substituted for the Eucharist on Sunday.

Eucharist & Office: The Ground

Our life in community, our reflection, and our service are nurtured from the soil of Office and Eucharist. The daily connection with Scripture and common prayer and the weekly receiving of Body and Blood orient us to the ways of eternity and feed us for "real life." St. Paul must have observed a comparable set of practices. Paul also knew that it all was God's doing. "Likewise the Spirit helps us in our weakness; for we do not know how to pray as we ought, but that very Spirit intercedes with sighs too deep for words. And God, who searches the heart, knows what is the mind of the Spirit, because the Spirit intercedes for the saints according to the will of God." (Romans 8: 26 – 27).

Any authentic priesthood must derive from an inner core of silence, a life hid with Christ in God ...Only those who are at home with silence and darkness will be able to survive in, and minister to, the perplexity and confusion of the modern world. Let us seek that dark silence out of which an authentic ministry and a renewed theology can grow and flourish.

Kenneth Leech, during the 1988 retreat
of the Order of the Ascension.

Four

Reflection—Inner Stillness and Silence Allowing Deep Listening

Our ability to be reflective depends on nurturing the inner life, on creating internal stillness and thereby a capacity to listen. While the quote from Father Leech on the facing page was addressed to a group of laity and priests; what he offered applies to us all. That interior silence is an essential element of the spiritual life of clergy and laity.

Our world is not one that encourages reflection. As the collect has it, "we are placed among things which are passing away," and we are "to hold fast to those that shall endure." Sorting one from the other is the work of reflection. It's all too easy to lose yourself. There's not some uncomplicated way to maintain a sense of perspective and moral vision. It calls for thought and discipline.

The traditional gifts of the Spirit and virtues (awe, courage, wisdom, justice, persistence and so on) are nurtured in all aspects of spiritual practice. But in our time it is our skill at reflection that may be most important in cultivating lives of integrity and harmony.

The fostering of such a life requires ways of reflecting that allow us:

- To see our experience in relationship to who we are as baptized members of the Body. For Anglicans this will mean reflection in relationship to the scriptures, the holy and catholic tradition, and reason.

- To discover what advances and what hinders our baptismal life.

- To learn from our reflection on experience.

53

- To act on those learnings with the behaviors of new life.

Four specific disciplines that may help are:

- Prayer that brings the stuff of our life into conscious relationship with Jesus Christ, in a manner that allows us to be reflective about our life, e.g., meditation, *lectio divina.*

- Spiritual guidance from other Christians. That can be accomplished in a variety of ways—a formal spiritual director relationship, working with another person in a peer spiritual friendship; it might be one-on-one or in a group; it could be a meeting of one hour or yearly retreat at a monastic house.

- Prayer that develops our capacity for stillness and silence. If we are to become more reflective about our experience we need to increase our ability to listen to God, others, and ourselves.

- Some method of self-examination, probably to include sacramental confession. Martin Thornton viewed the purpose of self-examination as aiming at *"tranquillitas,* not the suppression of desire, not *apatheia,* but harmony between the elements of personality."

Aspects of reflection

An integrated life in a fragmented world

Most of us wouldn't want a world with fewer choices. It was once the case that most people lived in homogeneous towns and neighborhoods in which just about everyone was the same religion and in which the expected behavior was obvious and reinforced by the culture.

That is still true in some parts of the world, but it's not where most Episcopalians live. We live in a world of choices. Choices are freeing and stressful at the same time. Choices fragment society as I go my way and you go your way. That doesn't mean we will want to give up the freedom that comes with choices.

How am I to have a sense of identity, integration and integrity in such a world? If the world isn't going to be organized in such a way that my life has a kind of built in integration, what am I to do?

I will need to accept responsibility for my life and that task. I will, as Thomas Merton puts it, have to work out my own identity in God, engage the effort of "working out salvation." [18] I will need to find my own way to Leech's "inner core of silence" and take on the struggle toward what he calls "the unifying of the personality, the integration of mind and heart into one center."[19]

To do that I will need to set my face to it. I can do it with companions—friends, the parish community, spiritual guides, and the whole company of heaven. I can make it easier by developing competencies in the spiritual life and emotional intelligence. But in the end the task of shaping an integrated life is an individual one. Others can't do it for me.

Living in the Presence

A fact of our lives is that we live in the presence of God; we are in Christ and Christ in us. This is true whether we have an awareness of it or not. Conscious awareness isn't even the goal. The objective is "a subconscious reliance upon God as members of the Body of Christ, in the workplace, family, friendship, civic life and congregational life." (See "Renewal—Apostolate Cycle" in the Resource section.)

Martin Thornton called this state habitual recollection. Others have called it holy worldliness, habitual grace, or "the practice of the presence of God."

That state is built up by grounding ourselves in Eucharist, Office, the community of the church, and particular methods of reflection and personal devotion.

Responsible action

Our grounding and patterns of reflection are finally to show themselves in practical action, something that is not as obvious as some think it should be.

Practical, responsible action is the outcome of a process: there's a bit of self awareness, attentiveness to what's happening around us, there's a capacity to understand what is important, there's an adequate ability to manage our own emotions and behavior, there's a life grounded in Mass and Office, and there's an openness to listening to voices other than our own. Of course, where that leads me may differ from where it leads you. I am to obey my informed conscience and you are to obey yours.

What issues from our status as baptized members of the Body is finally maturity and adulthood. That's because we are united with and incorporated into Christ, we share in the life of God; it's not that we are absorbed or taken over by Christ. For those who remember "Star Trek," this is not like the Borg assimilating species into a collective mind subservient to a monarch. The church's messages are "The glory of God is a human being fully alive," and "God became man so that man might become god,"[20] not "You will be assimilated" and "Resistance is futile."

The Christian path is about being responsible women and men. We have free will, wrestle with angles, ponder things, and make decisions. Bonhoeffer wrote of his faith, "I believe that even our errors and mistakes are turned to good account. ... I believe that God is no timeless fate but that he waits for and answers sincere prayer and responsible action." On the meaning of responsibility he wrote, "It depends upon a God who demands bold action as the free response of faith and who promises forgiveness and consolation to the man who becomes a sinner in the process."[21]

Martin Thornton acknowledged the toughness required: "Sane casuistry insists that circumstances alter cases, and it faces up to the facts of a world frequently demanding a choice of evils."[22] It's not that our effort to act responsibly will occasionally have us deciding between bad choices, but that it will happen frequently. This is partly a matter of what life presents. It's also that our vision is imperfect, we see dimly. [23]

As it is put in the Promise taken by members of the Order of the Ascension, we are "to seek the presence of Jesus Christ in the people, things and circumstances of life through stability, obedience and conversion of life." We do have the power to seek the Presence. We do have the power to give ourselves to stability, obedience and conversion of life. We don't have an ability to make it easy or to always get it right.

John Macquarrie wrote, "...our belief is that the whole process only makes sense in so far as, in the risk and the struggle of creation, that which *is* is advancing into fuller potentialities of being and is overcoming the forces that tend toward dissolution; and that continually a richer and more fully diversified unity is built up. ...The end, we have seen reason to believe, would be a commonwealth of free, responsible beings united in love; and this great end is possible only if finite existents are preserved in some kind of individual identity. Here again, we may emphasize that the highest love is not the drive toward union, but rather letting-be."[24]

Responsible action isn't primarily about the grand causes of life. It's largely about the routine stuff of going to work, caring for your friends and family, and being a good neighbor. The "commonwealth of free, responsible beings united in love" emerges from the stuff of daily life.

There is a conversation we each need to have with ourselves about what will satisfy us and how we get to that place. There's nothing wrong with playing video games, watching TV, reading mysteries, or eating candy. We all have activities that provide us with short-term pleasure. The problem comes when, in practice, we have substituted those things for shaping a life we love; when the short-term comfort is at the cost of a deeper and longer-term contentment. It's a form of reflection to have a talk with ourselves about our passion and hopes, our routines and commitments, our perseverance and stability.

Find Ourselves

Prayer must involve the unifying of the personality, the integration of mind and heart into one center.... Without self discovery there can be no further progress. 'In order to find God whom we can only find in and through the depths of our own soul, we must first find ourselves.' Without self-knowledge our love remains superficial.

Kenneth Leech, *Soul Friend*

There is a lifelong quest to become a person, to have Augustine's "real life." We Christians think it's an eternal journey. The assumption is that if we can become more self-aware of what we are thinking and feeling we will see more choices about how we live and deal with others. Understanding what we feel and why we feel that, where it comes from in us, gives us an opportunity to accept responsibility for and make improvements in our lives.

Columnist David Brooks suggested two ways in which people engage this process. He called the first "the Well Planned Life." In that way you work at finding an overall purpose and then based on that purpose make "decisions about allocating your time, energy and talent. The other he called "the Summoned Life." That route assumes that, "Life isn't a project to be completed; it is an unknowable landscape to be explored." You face the issues of life "primarily by sensitive observation and situational awareness, not calculation and long-range planning."[25] In either case we may move toward "the unifying of the personality, the integration of mind and heart into one center."

Silence and stillness

Man is what he does with his silence. Baron von Hugel

I recall a retreat with parishioners to Holy Cross Monastery in West Park in which one of the men from our group was so disturbed by the silence he would escape for long walks and much smoking. In the end, he would wander the countryside alone, in silence.

Silence terrifies many people and they will go to great lengths to banish it from their lives. At the same time, we long for silence. Our society has a tacit commitment to avoid silence and stillness. I'm certain that it will be easier to grow a parish's membership if we avoid having much silence in the Liturgy. I'm also convinced that our parishes will be unable to engage their primary work if they avoid silence. It's a spiritual practice that may offer us self-knowledge, an improved ability to engage our lives, and finally peace.

Developing a taste for and skill with stillness and silence is connected with much else in the spiritual life. Our capacity to be silent is directly related to our ability for attentive listening. Our silence is the ground for wonder and awe, which is in turn needed for faithful service.

When Terence Blanchard was working out the music for Spike Lee's "When the Levees Broke," he visited his mother at the home in New Orleans in which he had spent most of his childhood. As they stood in the doorway his mother cried and he saw that the "Levees" story was his story.

Larry Blumenfeld writing in the *Wall Street Journal* put what happened this way, "...[W]hen he sat down to translate his compositions for 'Levees' into a suite for jazz band and orchestra, he heard only silence. 'That's my memory of my visit to my mother's house,' he said. 'No cars. No birds, no insects. Nothing. But the silence finally broke, and I started to hear voices, and the stories those voices told. I tried to give the listener an idea of all this through my orchestration for the opening piece: The strings are the water; my trumpet, the cry for help that got no response for days.' He called the CD, 'A Tale of God's Will.' "[26]

Silence allows us to listen. Silence makes reflection possible. Silence allows us to hear the other voices.

Many people dread being silent. In some way we all fear it. In the silence, thoughts, feelings and images we find disturbing rise up. They may be about our temptations to rage, passivity, or inappropriate sexual expression. They may be about sin, things we have done, and left undone. Some take early note of their apprehension and avoid such experiences with activity and noise. The prayer of silence is to bring us into conformity with Christ; to draw us bit by bit into the very life of God. As the prayer puts it, "where we may be still and know that you are God." There is much to be faced on that journey. Our willingness to return to silence is our choosing to trust in God's love and mercy.

The parish can provide times of silence and stillness in the Eucharist and Office; a few minutes before beginning, a minute or two after a reading. Quiet days in Advent and Lent, or weekend retreats at a monastic house, can feed those ready for more silence.

Teaching methods of silent prayer can be part of a foundations course or school of prayer.

Reflection and passion

It is not to pleasant days and well fashioned lives and sheltered peace that Christ summons you, but to tears and the splendor of sacrifice, and the height and depth of lives lived in warfare, a world of wonder and joy, but of anguish and agony. Father John Neville Figgis, C. R. in the Cambridge Hulsean Lectures 1908)[27]

> *and before I could argue him*
> *out of his philosophy*
> *he went and immolated himself*
> *on a patent cigar lighter*
> *i do not agree with him*
> *myself I would rather have*
> *half the happiness and twice*
> *the longevity*
>
> *but at the same time I wish*
> *there was something I wanted*
> *as badly as he wanted to fry himself*
> "the lesson of the moth" by Don Marquis[28]

What are we to give our hearts to? What dream can shape our lives? The parish can nurture men and women to "desire a better country" and understand faith as "the assurance of things hoped for, the conviction of things not seen."

I'm writing this a day after Ted Kennedy's death. Senator Kennedy was the last of three famous brothers. They were Christians in the Irish Catholic tradition. Family and church shaped them to have large hearts and grand passions.

The problems of the world cannot possibly be solved by skeptics or cynics whose horizons are limited by the obvious realities. We need men who can dream of things that never were. John Kennedy

There are those who look at things the way they are, and ask why... I dream of things that never were, and ask why not? Robert Kennedy

For all those whose cares have been our concern, the work goes on, the cause endures, the hope still lives, and the dream shall never die.
Ted Kennedy

In life and death the Kennedys were criticized, by the small of heart on the left because they weren't perfect enough, and by the small of heart on the right because of what they championed. Their passion was about public service in the hope of a better country.

Our passions can be misdirected, being spent in unworthy or mistaken causes. They can be unfulfilled because we lack discipline or nerve. So, the parish's task is also to facilitate the kind of reflection that brings us to consider and develop those gifts and virtues that our passion requires: awe, courage, perseverance, practical judgment, and all the rest. In time we may grow and find the balance needed so our passion might be more productive.

Such growth occurs over time as we reflect on our experience. It comes in victories but maybe especially in our defeats. Ted Kennedy knew the sudden and violent death of all his brothers, his own near death in an airplane crash, divorce, the disgrace of Chappaquiddick, and the failure of his presidential aspirations. He also knew the value of friendship and family, the finding of a new love, and the place of the church and faith in life.

Kennedy attended Mass frequently, often several times a week. He was at Mass every day in the year after his mother died. He spent his last hours in prayer with a priest. A friend and neighbor on Cape Cod spoke of Kennedy's last year: "It was a bad diagnosis, but it allowed for the gift of reflection and some good times."

Adam Clymer wrote of how Kennedy began early on to develop the capacity to make his passions productive. "In 1965, his third year in office, he was senior to his older brother Robert, then a newly elected senator from New York, on the Committee on Labor and Public Welfare. One day they sat through a hearing, waiting for senior senators to finish their questions. Like a schoolboy bored in class, Robert passed Ted a note: 'Is this the way I become a good senator — sitting here and waiting my turn?' Ted scribbled, 'Yes.' Then Robert asked, 'How many hours do I have to sit here to be a good senator?' Ted replied, 'As long as necessary, Robbie.' "[29]

In one life we see elements of the map played out. The ground of Eucharist and prayer, integrated in community and reflection, issuing forth in service.

The opportunity for reflection

The vestry retreat started with dinner. Members had pulled together a variety of pasta dishes and salad. The priest stood with me off to the side as I snarfed the food. *Pretty good.* She told me how the parish was part of a network committed to the humane treatment of animals. *Nice!* They had decided that this Lent would be a meatless Lent. *Great!* Here was a very liberal parish engaged in practices that were popular in progressive circles and also very ancient and catholic.

When we moved into the exercise that would begin our weekend together I had each person do a self-assessment of their spiritual life and share what they were willing to share in a small group. After that we gathered as a whole group; I asked if anyone wanted to share what they were thinking and wondering. One person after another noted how they had lost track of spiritual practices that had made them more grounded.

The food was good. The meatless Lent in the service of the humane treatment of animals was good. What would have been missed if it had not been part of the weekend was an opportunity to assess our spiritual life and consider for yet another Lenten season how to re-ground ourselves in those practices that make for health and salvation.

How often do our parishes lose track of the basics and substitute something that in itself may be commendable but misses the deeper need?

The parish church needs to provide opportunities every year for parishioners to reflect on, assess, and shape their spiritual lives. It's not something most people will do on their own. Many don't know how to do it. We move through our days and years being managed by the built-in expectations and demands on our time. Our spiritual life is simply not urgent. It's important, but it's not urgent. It sits in the background of our thinking and imagining. It pops up occasionally in a groan or hunger, a longing or desire. Then it moves again into the background.[30]

The parish church is a community in the life of its members that can legitimately invite people to reflection and to a deeper spiritual life. We need to operate on the assumption that by virtue of their membership in the parish people have made at least a tentative invitation to engage them. We can provide the setting in which it will happen on a relatively superficial, but nonetheless significant, level for many. We can also have opportunities in which some will press deeper and by doing that enrich the whole.

How does reflection happen now?

William Temple said, "We must learn to pray as we are, not as we are not." While the Eucharist and Office are the ground for all of us, the prayer and practice of reflection will differ from one to another. Personality and temperament will orient us toward certain practices. Each needs settings that facilitate our capacity to think about things we have not thought about and to dream new dreams.

In classes and spiritual guidance the parish can help us look at a number of things. How do you reflect now? What are the ways in your life that you become centered and still? How do you gain a sense of perspective and proportion? In my own life this has frequently been connected to long walks in the city, a drink with a friend, and spiritual reading, often done with some work-related purpose in mind. I know that each practice may not offer anything useful for others. We each have our own way.

A member of my parish wrote about how it happens for her while hiking in the mountains. "Seeing the Earth from a different perspective and in such beauty shakes up stagnant thoughts that are weighing me down, brings up new observations, and opens my mind and soul to new ways."

We each need to find what works for us. In time, and with guidance, we can expand on how we reflect. Our parish church can help us explore all this.

It may also help to identify how we avoid reflection. We can use almost anything—work, general business, drugs, television, video games, alcohol, and sex can all be effective ways to evade reflection. Take care not to suggest that these things are problems in themselves. They can all add to the pleasure of life for some of us, at some times. The question is how they function in a particular life.

Methods

The parish has the opportunity to offer instruction and spiritual direction in the various methods of reflection. A module of the foundations course might focus on this. If there is a Sunday adult forum, at least a third of the programs could offer specific guidance in the spiritual practices of reflection. Over time many would increase their ability.

The starting place may be in helping members identify, affirm and improve ways that already work for them. Many will want to explore methods that are unfamiliar but for some reason attractive. Some may have so cluttered life with trivia and noise that they will need assistance in trying out various ways as they discover what may best fit their personality.

Lectio Divina

Praying the Scriptures and other spiritual writings is for many a way of nurturing a mindfulness of God; a way of being in conversation with God about the stuff of our life. It may be done alone or with others. This combination of meditation and reading is a way of increasing our awareness of God's presence in our life. At times to literally carry through our day "a word." Spiritual reading is about conversion of life with intellectual curiosity or development being either secondary or completely beside the point.

Reflection on experience

We need ways to learn from our experience. The parish can introduce members to various methods, including:

- Spiritual direction or guidance, either on a one-on-one basis or in a group

- Approaches to meditation or mental prayer that help connect the Scriptures or other spiritual readings to the experiences and patterns of our daily life.

- Therapy has been critical for many. Cognitive therapy seems to be very useful in helping people understand the mental frames, ways of thinking, that shape how they understand their experience.

- Writing in the form of keeping a journal or as part of a writing project that explores your life and issues of spiritual and emotional growth.

The usefulness of these methods will depend on our skill in reflecting upon and learning from experience. Reflection is a competency we can develop. This might be learned in therapy or spiritual direction, depending on the approach of a therapist or director. A learning method that is specifically geared for such learning is lab training.[31]

Lab training and other forms of experiential education have used a very disciplined three-step method.

- **Identify** an experience that seems significant for you; note what happened.

- **Analyze** the experience, possibly looking at the impact or result, maybe using a theory of model, certainly noting your feelings and thoughts and how you managed them.

- **Generalize** by saying what you might do in a similar situation; ways in which you might try new behavior. Generalizing specifically opens up awareness of options for the future.

An effective way of learning this method so it might be used in the parish is to attend lab training. In recent years Roy Oswald has worked with others in offering "Emotional Intelligence – Human Relations" labs. Another group, LTI (Leadership Training Institute),[32] has used the same methods in providing labs in human interaction, educational design skills, conflict management, community building, group development, and consultation skills. Michelle Heyne and I have recently designed "Shaping the Parish™,"[33] a parish revitalization program that works with leaders in the areas of: spiritual practice, emotional and social intelligence, and change theory and methods. The learning process is largely one of learning from disciplined reflection on the experience of participants in the workshop and the parish.

Our ability to learn from experience requires two primary things. We need the competence to do it. That's where lab training can be so useful. We need to understand the process not merely as written but as a human interaction. We also need other people to support and challenge us. Friends, co-workers, spiritual directors and therapists, other participants in a training program, all can offer feedback, and tell us the impact we have on them, the working group and the larger system.

It's difficult to get perspective on ourselves without some skill at self-awareness and reflection. We need others to help us see what is hidden to us but seen by them. Growing in wisdom entails an inner silence, competence in reflection, and others to nudge us toward out true life.

Personal devotions

There are in the church's tradition thousands of practices used to help people become more centered and attentive or to connect the stuff of daily life with the movement of the Spirit. These methods may be very useful for some people as a kind of backdrop for reflection.

For others they may become a problem. Some allow themselves to become overwhelmed by taking on too many of these practices. Others may become erratic as they flit from one to another. Many people find their life enriched when they find a few practices that are especially aligned with their temperament and need.

The tradition of personal devotions includes everything from contemplation to saying the rosary to thanksgiving at meals. One way of categorizing personal devotions is:

- **Acts of recollection.** This may be a spontaneous, unexpected awareness of God's presence or the movement of the Spirit. Or it may be habits taken on to recall God's presence in certain situations. So, some say grace at meals or offer a prayer or cross themselves when they hear the siren of an emergency vehicle. Prayer beads may be used to center a person into a stance of recollection. I have used phrases of short verses to the same effect. One of my favorites is something I picked up in the work of Alan Jones:

> *To see thee is the End and*
> *the Beginning*
> *Thou carriest me and*
> *thou goest before*
> *Thou art the journey*
> *and the journey's End*
> -Attributed to King Alfred

- **Colloquy.** Discussion or dialogue with God. This is what many are referring to when they speak of "saying their prayers."
- **Mental prayer.** Including methods of meditation, contemplation and spiritual reading.

Parishioners often need guidance in understanding the role of personal devotions in the spiritual life. They may take on an overblown importance for a person because they are so connected to personal choice, hopefully aligned with personality, and frequently have roots in childhood. These practices can provide such comfort they end up inhibiting the development of a more balanced, efficient, and effective spiritual life.

The parish priest needs to remind people of two realities:

1) The grounding is to be in the weekly practice of the Eucharist and the daily practice of the Prayers of the Church.

2) Efficiency is a useful measure in spiritual life. *More* pious activity isn't necessarily better. The question is, "What practices are necessary to provide a conscious and intentional attention to God and our status as baptized people in order to make possible an effective subconscious reliance upon God in our daily life in the workplace, family, friendship, and civic life?"

Threads of wisdom

Many threads of wisdom have informed our Anglican tradition. Individual personalities may find it easier to connect to one more then another; some Celtic, others Franciscan. Julian of Norwich and the anchorite and solitary tradition have touched some, the Evangelical and Anglo-Catholic movements have fed others. Any of these may serve the spiritual inclinations of a person, provide comfort and support, offer paths in which to walk and grow.

The heart of the tradition is Benedictine—the threefold Rule of Prayer (Eucharist, Office, Personal Devotions) explicit and implicit in the Prayer Book; the assumption of a spirituality for all the baptized as part of an inclusive and cohesive community; a sense that spiritual growth is toward living in Christ; what has been called habitual recollection or holy worldliness; and a gentle, stable, and familial orientation regarding spiritual discipline and parish life. Regardless of what other spiritualities feed us we do well to give ourselves to that primary way.

God has so ordained things that we grow in faith only through the frail instrumentality of one another.

John of the Cross

Five

Participating in Community

Participation in the parish community is a spiritual practice that can further our personal growth and integrate life.

The parish as community

The parish church is a community. More correctly, in most cases it is several communities or congregations. If we look at what is possible in a Christian community it becomes clear that we need to think in terms of the community people see themselves as part of. For most that's likely to be a circle within the particular group they worship and have coffee with on Sunday, the 8:00 or 10:00 congregation, as well as the total parish community.

The Scriptures are filled with the theme of the possibilities in community:

> "love one another with mutual affection; outdo one another in showing honor." (Romans. 12:10); "live in harmony with one another" (Romans. 12:16); "Welcome one another, therefore, just as Christ has welcomed you, for the glory of God." (Romans 15:7); "you yourselves are full of goodness, filled with all knowledge, and able to instruct one another." (Romans 15:14); "when you come together to eat, wait for one another." (1 Corinthians 11:33); "through love, be servants of one another" (Galatians 5:13); "encourage one another and build up each other" (1 Thessalonians. 5:11); "with all humility and gentleness, with patience, bearing with one another in love," (Ephesians 4:2); "be kind to one another, tender-hearted, forgiving one another" (Ephesians 4:32); "be subject to one another out of reverence for Christ" (Ephesians. 5:21); "confess your sins to one another, and

> pray for one another" (James 5:16); "clothe yourselves, all of you, with humility towards one another" (1 Peter 5:5); "we have fellowship with one another" (1 John 1:7); "So let us not grow weary in doing what is right, ... whenever we have an opportunity, let us work for the good of all, and especially for those of the family of faith." (Galatians 6:9-10); "that they may be one, as we are one" (John 17:11); "Love is patient; love is kind; love is not envious or boastful or arrogant or rude. It does not insist on its own way; it is not irritable or resentful; it does not rejoice in wrongdoing, but rejoices in the truth. It bears all things, believes all things, hopes all things, endures all things." (1 Corinthians 13: 1 -7); "If another member of the church sins against you, go and point out the fault when the two of you are alone. If the member listens to you, you have regained that one. But if you are not listened to, take one or two others along with you ..." (Matthew 18:15-17); "Above all, maintain constant love for one another, for love covers a multitude of sins. Be hospitable to one another without complaining. Like good stewards of the manifold grace of God, serve one another with whatever gift each of you has received." (1 Peter 4:8-10)

The parish community is a gift of God. It's a pathway into communion with God and our sisters and brothers. In that community we can come to know and love God, become friends of God and of one another.

As has been noted earlier, the base is Eucharist and Office. Community is built on the foundation of the Church's liturgy that in weekly and daily practice maintains and restores our participation in the life of God in word and sacrament.

Our personal and spiritual growth is bound up with being in community. Dietrich Bonhoeffer put it this way: "The new person is like a garment made to cover the individual believer...It is impossible to become a new person as a solitary individual. The new person is not the individual believer after he has been justified and sanctified, but the Christian community, the Body of Christ, Christ himself."

Parker Palmer wrote, "Community is that place where the person you least want to live with always lives...And when that person moves away, someone else arrives immediately to take his or her place." That's a reminder that there is no perfect community in this life. The parish is built with the stuff of human frailty. The heavenly Jerusalem is something we taste now and know fully in the future.

We need images of what a healthy parish community looks like and we need methods that foster the marks of such communities. If we are to grow as sisters and brothers we need to engage the qualities and patterns that build that relationship. There are qualities to nurture such as kindness, respect, self-control, humor, and generosity. There are also communal patterns to develop such as balance, mutual obedience and trust, discipline, face-to-face encounter, full and deep listening and dialogue.

Images of health

A participant in the Church Development Institute (CDI) responded to a presentation on spiritual practices with the admission that she didn't have an image of what a healthy parish looked like. This was a priest who had been badly hurt in her last parish community. She knew she had a problem. How could she help shape it if she didn't know what "health" looked like?

How many parish leaders don't have an image of health? I've come across many who use sentimental or overly broad statements of values to cover the fact that they don't have such an image. They speak of parishes being safe or comfortable. They talk about a variety of programs and ministries they associate with a successful parish. Some focus on membership growth. There's nothing wrong with any of that. It's just not a description of a healthy community.

It reminded me of what David Cooperrider, creator of Appreciative Inquiry, experienced when he worked with a two star hotel. The method he was using asked people to identify what was already present in the organization that could be expanded and built upon. In this case there was just too little to work with. There was nothing worthy to expand and build upon.[34]

Some parishes are one or two star parishes. They have lost track of what provides roots and wings in life. Some are three star parishes that have "settled" or may want more but are unwilling to venture in the new directions that will take them there. Others are fixated on false measures such as size. Understanding what a 4 or 5 star parish looks like is critical to making changes in that direction.

What are some of the characteristics of a healthy community?

There are odd people

Flannery O'Conner wrote, "You shall know the truth and the truth shall make you odd." As our parish lives in the Truth, we will become more and more ourselves, which is to say odder and odder. The parish can be a place that supports us along our own irreplaceable journey as we develop into a unique self with a full life.

In another sense of "odd" I'm referring to people who are different from us. They don't see things the way we do. They live in a manner that is foreign to us. Even in what may appear to be a rather homogenous parish community there are enough differences to stretch our capacity for acceptance and offer us ways to learn the mysteries of self and community.

For fifteen years I had a consulting contract with WomenRising, a Jersey City agency with programs in employment, economic development, domestic abuse, and affordable housing. It was a broad organization development effort around increasing productivity and quality in their service to others, quality of work life, employee empowerment, and teamwork. The roughly 80 full time staff members were mostly Latino and African American women, some white women, and a few men.

74

They had the usual tensions between racial and ethnic groups, but something I heard over and over was that the most difficult differences to cope with were things like these: having to share work space with people who were more extraverted or introverted than you were; or the different ways people perceived things (more concrete vs. more in terms of possibilities); or how others made decisions (more rational and logical versus more based on feelings and gut instinct.)

These day-by-day encounters in which they came up against these "odd others" were for many young women opportunities to grow in understanding, empathy and wisdom.

We haven't chosen one another and because of that there may be more opportunities for "bearing with one another in love, making every effort to maintain the unity of the Spirit in the bond of peace" or "Forbearing one another in love." (Ephesians 4:2)

There's a shared way of being and a direction

K. H. Ting wrote, "Love is not something just to be enjoyed by two persons, you and me. Love means we have the same orientation, look toward the future together and step forward together. It is this kind of love which is adequate to enable people to be mutually encouraged, mutually spurred on, mutually supportive, and together become co-partakers in God's creative process."[35]

In *Fill All Things* I proposed the Shape of the Parish model as a way think about how a parish could have a common life and direction while being made up of people with various levels of spiritual maturity. (See Resource section for a diagram and more explanation of the model.) The assumptions of that approach are seen in other places:

- "Critical mass theories are used by many Organization Development practitioners. The model suggests building the level of commitment, competence and emotional maturity at the center of the organization so that it

75

grounds the system in a mission orientation and an organizational culture that supports the mission. The grounding then is enfleshed; made real in the lives of men and women. It's in the habits of people rather than statements of leaders."[36]

- You can see the same orientation when Bishop Kilmer Myers wrote, "One of the main tasks of the parish priest is to train the militant core of his parishioners in such a way that they understand as fully as possible the true nature of a Christian parish." [37]

- In *Pastoral Theology: A Reorientation* Martin Thornton presented his understanding of the parish church as the Body of Christ, "the complete Body in microcosm," and his Remnant Concept, "in which power from the center pervades the whole." The holiness and love of a Remnant at the center of parish life is for Thornton what makes a parish a true parish.[38]

There's love

Bishop Myers also said that the story of every parish was to be a love story. The parish community lives in the love of God. It is in some measure a reflection of that community of love we call the Blessed Trinity. The Rule of the Society of Saint John the Evangelist says, "There is a ceaseless interchange of mutual love which unites the Father, Son, and Holy Spirit. The Orthodox have a beautiful image: they call it *perichoresis*, an eternal dance of love between the three persons of the Trinity." Our life as a parish partakes of that dance.

This truth about love in the parish needs to be kept in perspective and not idealized. In a gathering of clergy and lay leaders working on how to improve their parishes, one priest became agitated as people spoke of the complexities of acceptance and thought through their choices and how open they wanted to be with one another at this early stage of group life. Trying, probably unconsciously, to circumvent that process by reframing the issue as

76

a Christian "should," the priest said something along these lines: "We are all friends in Christ; so we should be open with one another, trust one another." Such romantic thinking only confuses things.

Acceptance trust and love are hard won victories for any community. Because it *can be* true doesn't make it a living reality in a particular parish community. Using words like "should" only adds a layer of judgment that gets in the way. Love and trust are developed by immersion in Eucharist and Office, by reflection, by giving ourselves to life in community, and as we create a life together.

In the end we do what we can, given what we are—"You shall love your crooked neighbor, with your crooked heart," wrote Auden.

To be a community of love is certainly a calling and possibility for any parish. The extent to which it is manifested in a particular parish is related to the presence of people of Apostolic Faith, and a parish climate and way of life that is itself apostolic. It will be hindered to the extent that those of a more tentative and immature faith control the emotional center of the parish. [39]

Still, the parish church can be a "school of love." It can be a community in which people experience love and learn to love. The extent to which that potential is achieved will depend in large part upon its being a community grounded in weekly and daily practice, reflective about its whole life, including the ways of love in community, and given to service.

Leaders can help by deciding that the starting point is in their own willingness to be committed to the well being of others. This is a decision rather than a feeling. Yes, the parish is a community of love. It is a community that has a calling to decide again and again to actively seek the well being of other people.

As with all communities, that love is manifested in the face of jealously and resentments, pride and self-serving behavior. So we repent and return to the decision.

We are able to have a stance of love toward God and all people in general. From that orientation, enhanced or limited by our temperament, we are able to routinely show love to the individuals we encounter in life.

There's hospitality-as-formation

The hospitality of a parish community is directed at the neighborhood or community in which it exists, those who might consider membership, the visitor—stranger, and its own members.

There is a form of hospitality to offer the community in which the parish exists. It's not simply about serving the community. It's more about being a responsible institution in the town or neighborhood. It's a form of stewardship as we care for the community in which we are set or with which we have a significant relationship. For most parishes that will be a geographical area. On occasion it will be with a community of people. For example I was once vicar in a parish with a relationship with the jazz and performing arts community.

There is also the hospitality we offer those who might in time become part of our parish community. This is the hospitality of formation, formation rather than welcome. We need to be clear about what we are up to here.

It's not the hospitality of having a guest over for dinner or the hospitality of a good hotel or restaurant. It's more like the hospitality the Marine Corps shows a new recruit (although not, of course, in the actual practices of yelling commands and shaving heads). The Marine Corps, along with other defined organizations have a rationale of engaging people new to the organization with an eye to the person's formation.

If we are to form a Marine, or a good teacher or nurse, or a carpenter, we do things at the front-end so we increase the likelihood that they will be good at being a Marine, teacher, nurse or carpenter. This understanding of "front-end" action was one of the significant learnings of the quality improvement movement.

In the parish we can offer a hospitality that will orient the new member toward their growth in Christian maturity. In doing that we'll take into account where people are in their own journey. How are we to engage someone who is tentative and immature in Christian practice versus one who is transferring into the parish, or coming from another communion, and is already proficient? The hospitality we offer depends on the person's real needs and specific place in the Body of Christ.

So, hospitality is a phase of incorporation into membership. More accurately, it is a phase into full, mature membership. And mature membership, in turn, is about human maturity. Our invitation is into maturity, into "real life." The hospitality of the parish is to be done in such a manner that a person might finally come to "real life."

At the front-end of this act of hospitality-as-formation there is a paradoxical dynamic. We are to welcome new people without imposing our views on them. We are to welcome, love and support them freely, without conditions. In this parish they are offered a space in which to be and grow. There's no rush. They may be part of this community's life as they are. Our stance is one of receptivity and openness.

Along with this stance of acceptance there is also a confrontation. As individuals and as a community we have come to certain values and ways of doing things. We carry in us deep assumptions about the nature of things, what God is up to, how a person becomes fully alive, the nature and purpose of the church. In an open, non-aggressive manner we are to share those things with the new person. We are to share ourselves. That is a form of confrontation.

To do hospitality well we need to understand the dynamics of inclusion. Inclusion is a two-way process. The person new to the community has to decide to include herself.

"Welcome" is not the same as inclusion. Inclusion is a complex process in which the person new to the community becomes incorporated in the ways of the community. Everyone may be welcomed and the parish can unilaterally accept responsibility for welcoming.

"Inclusion," however, involves the movement of *both the community and the person.* There are all the initial matters of inclusion described by William Schutz involving questions of cost and trust. What does it cost to be part of this community? Can I trust myself to these people? And the reverse—can we trust this new person among us? What will it cost us to have them be part of our life? The process of inclusion continues as the concerns of control and influence, openness, affection and intimacy are engaged and adequately resolved.

The life of this parish community is worthwhile as it is. The visitor is welcome to join in and taste it but the life is not twisted in an attempt to make the visitor comfortable. In any case, our attempts to make visitors "comfortable" may just as easily cause them discomfort.

We can offer people acceptance of who and how they are right now. We can love people as they are. If that love is to be anything other than sentimentality and feel-good, however, it needs to also be an invitation into a transformed and new life. Paul wrote about putting away our old self and putting on a new self "created according to the likeliness of God." (Ephesians 4: 22 – 24)

There are friendships

> *We are created to be God's friends. God made us for that. Christ lived and died as one of us, and went into heaven to take our humanity into the very life of God, that we might become God's friends. Christian community in general, and your form of it in particular, is made for friendship, and by friendship. We are to foster friendship with God by being friends ourselves.*
>
> Father Emmett Jarrett[40]

Friendships in the parish are inevitable, life enhancing and part of how the parish grows in grace.[41] John Henry Newman wrote, "The love of our private friends is the only preparatory exercise for the love of all men." We learn to love by loving.

People with friendships are more resilient and seem to have more of a capacity for perseverance and empathy, all of which are traits helpful in a parish's life.

Relationships that are especially close, such as friendships and families, also create potential problems in the parish. The strong connection between two friends or among family members will come into play in the parish's political and social life. These alliances can coalesce in resistance to needed changes or can be a force for that change. They will also set off jealousy in some of the more immature members. The spiritual practice of the parish community is partly one of supporting friendships but it's also one of learning to manage the sometimes problematic dynamics set loose around those friendships.

Some of these friendships may be especially close and intense. The biblical examples of Jonathan and David, Ruth and Naomi, Mary Magdalene and Jesus, and Jesus and John point to our capacity for a deep love that is a participation in God's friendship with humanity.

In their parish friendships clergy have an opportunity to fully participate in the community's life and to experience the deep pleasure possible in friendship. It's an opportunity to be known as a person. The issue of bonding between priest and people in the parish moves toward a kind of fulfillment when the priest is accepted as both symbol and person.[42]

There's a climate of acceptance and challenge

People grow in communities in which they experience both acceptance and challenge. If the parish is all "acceptance" people sink into the bland life that offers. If it's too much "challenge" people become fearful or judgmental. The norm might be "we accept you as you are and we invite you to become more than you

81

are now." There needs to be an invitation to grow, to experience that a full life is more than what they have imagined.

Two images of what acceptance and challenge look like:

1) A member comes to the vicar and says, "Father, I can't keep up with all the page turning in the Prayer Book (or leaflet). Would you please announce all page numbers so it's easier for me? I'd appreciate it so much." The acceptance/challenge response might be, "Let me help you with that in another way. Let's sit down and I'll show you the flow and rhythm of the liturgy. And if that doesn't work for you I can help you look at the spiritual life opportunity in this. Allowing yourself to rest in the community; allowing yourself to let go of fear and anxiety about getting things right."

2) On Maundy Thursday, dealing with the discomfort of some people about having their feet washed by allowing them to have their discomfort. Washing another's feet is an act of humility and service. The clergy washing the feet of parishioners is a model of the humility and service we are each invited to in daily life. However, the primary issue of spiritual life for most people isn't about being willing to serve others (wash the feet of others) but about allowing someone to wash their feet. "Peter said to him, 'You will never wash my feet.' Jesus answered, 'Unless I wash you, you have no share with me.' "

Some clergy take away this invitation by explicitly saying, "It's acceptable to come to have your feet washed or not. Either is just fine." That's simply not true. An acceptance/challenge message might be something like this, "Christ Jesus and His Body the Church, invite you to have your feet washed. This spiritual practice is a profound way of sharing in the life of Christ and the Church." Let it stand at that. We aren't going to force it upon people. It is an invitation they may accept when they are ready.

People touch

Touch is innately humanizing. Jesus healed with his touch. Thomas believed through touching. Many doctors know about touch. The routine of using the stethoscope and pressing the patient's belly may be less about diagnostic benefits and more because it's expected and also because it makes a connection and offers comfort.[43] At coffee hour you'll see people hugging, patting a back, reaching across a table to grasp a hand.

Physical touch is a common element of liturgy. In the Eucharist we exchange the peace. At our baptism we are anointed and crossed with oil. On Ash Wednesday the cross is made on us with ashes. On Maundy Thursday there is foot washing. When we've ill there is the laying on of hands with anointing. All this touching is an expression of our communion with one another and God.

We also touch things—we eat bread and drink wine, we touch the water in the baptismal font.

> Captain Jean-Luc Picard: *It's a boyhood fantasy...I must have seen this ship hundreds of times in the Smithsonian but I was never able to touch it.*
>
> Lieutenant Commander Data: *Sir, does tactile contact alter your perception?*
>
> Captain Jean-Luc Picard: *Oh Yes! For humans, touch can connect you to an object in a very personal way.* (From *Star Trek: First Contact*)

Touching, as with most spiritual practices, requires us to exercise our emotional and social intelligence. Even though touching is normative in the church, there are those who, for various reasons, are unable to be touched even if the intention is to encourage, connect, or support. We are called to be aware and respectful.

Being in close proximity with others, and engaging in activities

83

such as the Peace, involves risk. We exchange germs, we may feel uncomfortable, or inadvertently cause someone else to feel uncomfortable. There is always some risk that comes with taking part in the liturgy. There is no way for to live in a germ-free, risk-free society. In fact we need one another's germs to establish an adequate immune system.

In healthy parishes we touch and are sensitive about how we do that.

We fight with those we love

A healthy community has fights. I believe that in general a community that faithfully engages the weekly and daily practices, is reflective and has an orientation toward serving, will have disagreements and conflicts that are relatively productive. Some group development theories note the necessity for working through issues of control and influence or "storming" before being able to become open enough with one another to be fruitful.

We do not judge each other

Welcome those who are weak in faith, but not for the purpose of quarreling over opinions. Some believe in eating anything, while the weak eat only vegetables. Those who eat must not despise those who abstain, and those who abstain must not pass judgment on those who eat; for God has welcomed them. ...We do not live to ourselves, and we do not die to ourselves. If we live, we live to the Lord, and if we die, we die to the Lord; so then, whether we live or whether we die, we are the Lord's. For to this end Christ died and lived again, so that he might be Lord of both the dead and the living. Why do you pass judgment on your brother or sister? Or you, why do you despise your brother or sister? For we will all stand before the judgment seat of God.

Rom. 14: 1- 3 and 5 - 10 (NRSV)

We do need to sort out the fact that judgment and challenge are different things. The parish does need to challenge and invite people to full maturity. It doesn't need to judge people.

The challenge comes primarily by being a community living by Rule—in Eucharist and Office, in Community and Reflection, and in Service. That life as lived in a parish church, in combination with the example and prayers of the all-too-fallible saints of the church, is the challenge needed. The world is challenged by a community struggling to love and forgive, be humble and courageous.

The problem is that many of our parishes see judging others and each other as acceptable and challenge as something to be avoided. Many feel safer that way.

A starting point may be to teach members a few basic communication skills, especially how to be open in self-disclosure and how to offer useful feedback. Judgment is when we have the thought that the other person is a fool. Challenge and feedback is when we can say, "When you take a lot of time at meetings offering ideas that I disagree with I feel upset and agitated." Or "When you dismiss what I say in response to your ideas I feel discounted and diminished."

There's tradition

Richard Fabian wrote in the *Plan for the Mission of St. Gregory of Nyssa in 1977,* "Christian tradition is the sharing of a journey. Its purpose is not to preserve our experience, but to enrich it with the experience of those before us and beside us who approach our common end from different directions. This is its purpose for individuals, who further their own journey by sharing in the company and common life of the Church. This is also its purpose for each of the churches, whom it guides and quickens by the vision of God in the others."

There's the Holy Catholic Church

Alice Mann of Alban Institute, wrote, "We have a communal relationship with God that both embodies and transcends all our individual faith journeys."[44] Common life, common prayer, and communal discernment are the starting place. It is from that place that we become the unique beings we are called to be.

We can invite members to affirm and know that there will be moments when they experience an eternal and broader dimension to being part of parish community. Russell Kirk thought T.S. Eliot said something like that. "Through the whole of Eliot's writing there was the idea of a community of souls; a bond of love and duty joining all the living, and also those who have preceded us and those who will follow us in the moment of time."[45]

We can invite them to know and thereby understand the moments when they sense being part of something much larger than this parish community. This parish community is a microcosm of the Holy Catholic Church. All the marks of the Church are alive in this parish community. It is not just that the larger church is one, holy, catholic and apostolic. This local church community is also one, holy, catholic and apostolic. The life of the Holy Spirit is the parish's life—a larger communion of the living and the dead, forgiveness, resurrection, and life everlasting.

There's caring for one another

I didn't know John very well. I knew who he was and we had some contact around the parish newsletter that he edited. After my surgery John came frequently to help cope with my own limits. I could do many things for myself but I didn't have the strength to do all of them. So, John and others would visit and make things easier for me. I recall him changing overhead light bulbs, going food shopping, doing laundry and going with me for walks. John, Kathie, Michelle, Meg, Jo, all from Trinity, were part of my "care team."

There were also people from other parishes like John C-M and Bryan, there were friends like Amanda and Lauren, and there were neighbors like Toni, who provided companionship and practical assistance in the months of recovery. Others offered prayer and on the occasions I could get to the Eucharist there was kindness and inquiries about how I was doing.

It's not that all such support comes from the church. It is true that a healthy parish stands alongside others in providing caring and support. In organized and informal ways parish churches often provide pastoral support, intercessory prayer, and rides to worship.

Other marks of a healthy parish

There are many other ways of describing the marks of a healthy parish community.

Based on the baptismal rite

We want to shape a parish community that has "an inquiring and discerning heart, the courage to will and to persevere, a spirit to know and to love you, and the gift of joy and wonder in all your works."

Based on the Creed

We want to shape a parish community that people experience as a microcosm of the whole church—one, holy, catholic, apostolic.

Based on the Ephesians and Galatians

We want to shape a parish community that has the characteristics listed in Ephesians of humility, gentleness, patience, forbearance born of love, eagerness to maintain unity in the bond of peace, truthfulness mediated in love, mutual kindness, tenderheartedness and forgiveness; and in Galatians of love, joy, peace, patience, kindness, generosity, faithfulness, gentleness and self-control.

Based on tradition

We want to shape a parish community that exhibits the theological virtues of faith, hope and love and the cardinal virtues of prudence, justice, fortitude and temperance. A community open to the gifts of the Holy Spirit[46] of fear (wonder and awe), piety (affection or reverence), knowledge or understanding, courage, counsel (right judgment), understanding, and wisdom.

Based on the research on emotional intelligence

We want to shape a parish community that enables:

1) Self-awareness (emotional self-awareness, accurate self- assessment, and self-confidence);

2) Self-management (Self-control, trustworthiness, conscientiousness, adaptability, achievement orientation, and initiative);

3) Social awareness (empathy, organizational awareness, service orientation); and

4) Social skill (visionary leadership, influence, developing others, communication, change catalyst, conflict management, team work and collaboration)

All these characteristics are compatible and mutually reinforcing. In some cases they can be intentionally nurtured and developed. In other cases we receive them as gifts, our role being to open ourselves to the gifts.

Theory and methods[47]

Scott Peck's Stages

Scott Peck developed an approach to community building that assumes four psychological stages leading to a cohesive group with high trust and a strong sense of connection. In *Working Together in Schools*, Gordon Donaldson and David Sanderson express Peck's stages this way.

1. **Pseudo-Community.** As it forms, the group pretends it already has found community. It can do so only by ignoring the differences in the group, thus hoping to avoid conflict. Politeness is the (unspoken) rule.

2. **Chaos.** As the group allows differences to emerge, individuals struggle to abolish them by winning, choosing "right" and "wrong," converting each other, and getting

nowhere. Conflict in this stage is uncreative and unproductive, yet members are beginning to open up and are no longer pretending.

3. **Emptiness.** As the bridge between chaos and community, "emptiness" signifies the transformational stage in which members let go of whatever has thus far kept the group from its real work: the preconceptions, prejudices, agendas, and other barriers to true communication that all members have brought to the group. Peck calls this action the group's "emotional surrender."

4. **Community.** This stage often begins with a sense of quiet peace. With genuine safety established, members feel free to be themselves, speaking and listening fully and authentically. The group is ready, at last, to work, to make decisions, to tackle solutions.

This model is about the process of moving from one place to a better place, from pseudo-community to community. I also find it useful to see this as a spectrum.

Pseudo-Community. Pretends it already has found community. Ignores differences, thus hoping to avoid conflict. Politeness is the (unspoken) rule.				Community. Genuine safety, members feel free to be themselves, speaking and listening fully and authentically.	
1	2	3	4	5	6

When viewed this way we can acknowledge that a community may be someplace in between the two positions. Many parishes are like that. There's some ability to be yourself, to speak and listen fully and authentically. It may be very sporadic. It may be in pockets in which some groups in the parish have developed a deeper and fuller community life while most of the parish is stuck in tentative relationships and working hard to avoid stepping on one another's toes.

Most parishes that I've had contact with live someplace between the two poles. They may not be able to bring themselves to do the hard work to shape and solidify a truly productive community but they are also not trapped in the pretense of "pseudo-community."

Few claim to have developed a "Community" on the occasions when I've used the model to have parish leaders look at their parish. They don't pretend to have "found Community." Some speak of chaos or emptiness, seeing their parish as "on the way." Others have more of the spectrum approach seeing their parish as someplace between the poles but also not really moving toward a better community life.

These parishes can be helped to move toward a better community life by leaders with the kind of skills and knowledge gained in programs like Shaping the Parish™ and the Church Development Institute. It's hard, complex work. It does require competencies that aren't learned in seminary or vestry training programs. In the case of clergy, these competencies may best be learned sometime in their first few years of being "in-charge" of a parish). The stages of chaos and emptiness could be managed with abilities and a stance that could be learned in a couple of years.

I've also experienced a few parishes that had what struck me as a pathological form of Pseudo-Community. There was in each case some awful experience and pain, unacknowledged, that was part of their history—for one it was how they dealt with their rector when his son was dying of cancer, for another it was racism, and in a third situation it was a long term pattern of sexual abuse.

Addressing these long-standing problems was difficult and required significant, intentional work. In all these cases the Chaos stage was intense and traumatic. What emerged after several years were parish communities that were utterly new. Much of the old congregation was gone and the parish culture was totally changed.

There are other parishes that have an investment in claiming a stronger and healthier parish community life than in fact exists. It's not that the parish has some deep pathology, though there may be some significant wound. That woundedness can be used in an attempt to protect "our community" against those who are "other" or who don't understand us. Of course it fails. But while in-play the parish expends a lot of energy maintaining the illusion of what a wonderful community it is.

What's tricky in such cases is that there is some truth about what a good community it is. There really is something wonderful there. The problem is that the need to claim more than exists comes at the cost of defensiveness and denial of differences.

Peck;s stages are similar to many of the group and trust development models used in organization development work.

Trust development [48]

We trust parish communities that exhibit certain characteristics.

- Reliability. We see consistency and dependability

- Responsiveness. There is sensitivity and empathy, an awareness of needs and openness to take action; my feelings are validated if not shared, my ideas will be respectfully responded to with dialogue, agreement and disagreement.

- Reciprocity. There is mutual exchange; I am fed and I feed others.

- Congruence. There's a feeling of harmony and unity; this community is what it claims to be.

91

The model I've worked with suggests four phases in trust development. My assumption is that the above characteristics become stronger as each phase develops.

1. Inclusion & Acceptance

2. Open Information

3. Shared Direction

4. Internal Commitment, Collaboration, Self-management

A parish that has a high level of commitment, collaboration and self-management can be said to be a parish that has a high trust level. The trust becomes visible in that way.

The parish always has the potential to develop and strengthen these four basic qualities of community life. These qualities "build" on each other in a sort of hierarchy, those near the bottom forming a "foundation" for the "higher" ones.

4. Internal Commitment, Collaboration, Self-management
3. Shared Direction
2. Open Information
1. Inclusion & Acceptance

For the community to become healthier and more trusting certain concerns related to each phase must be adequately resolved. Some of the concerns to be resolved as we build trust include:

4. Internal Commitment, Collaboration, Self-management		The extent to which: 1) direction and related decisions have internal commitment, a commitment not easily changed under pressure; 2) members are open to mutual influence from one another and see themselves as mutually accountable; 3) increased authority comes from increased competence, commitment, and spiritual and emotional maturity.
3. Shared Direction		The community's direction is shared, broadly owned. The direction is based on having explored options, is a free choice and not coming from coercion or habit, and is renegotiable if new information arises.
2. Open Information		The extent to which there is an open climate in which people feel free to share their feelings and ideas. That information is shared in a timely, useful, thorough and respectful manner.
1. Inclusion & Acceptance		How much do people in the parish community accept that others in the community belong and bring something to contribute? To what extent do people accept the parish's ways of being and doing, its espoused values and deeper underlying assumptions about God, humanity and the church, e.g., the culture?

As the concerns toward the base begin to be resolved, a foundation is built for resolving the concerns of the next phase. We can picture this as building blocks.

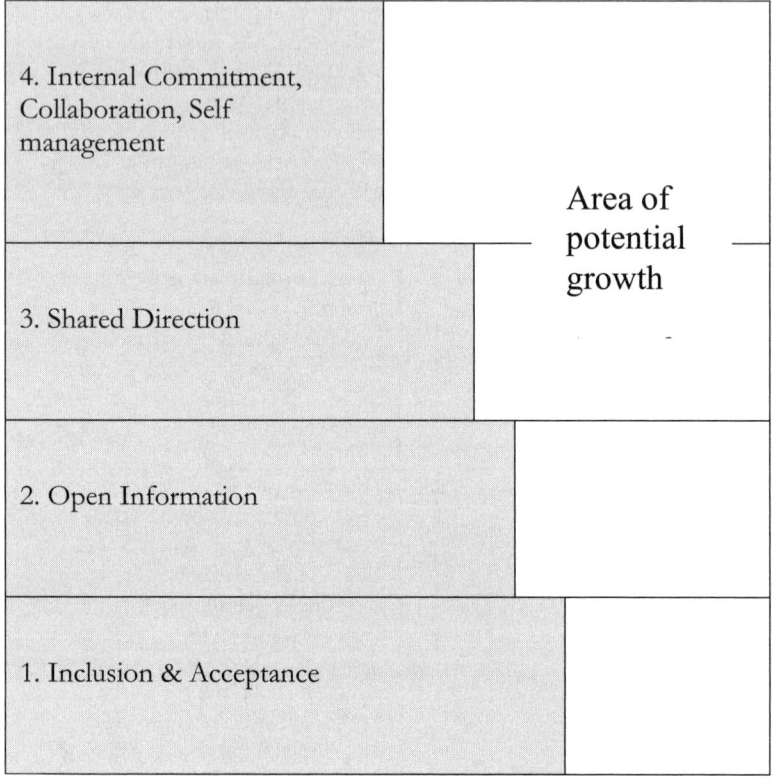

To the extent the inclusion and acceptance concerns have been resolved, members will feel free to be more open in sharing their feelings and thoughts about the community's life and work.

To the extent the community is sharing useful information it will have the base it needs for setting direction and making decisions. This open flow of information will generate the options about the direction and way of life for the community.

The extent to which members experience a sense of choice in exploring these options will determine the degree of internal commitment they have toward the direction and culture of the parish community.

When the community neglects the need for adequate resolution of "prior" concerns before taking on later concerns, an unstable relationship is the likely result. The blocks are likely to topple over! This is why things fall apart when leaders try to produce commitment and collaborative action by pressure, and insisting that we need 100% commitment from everyone.

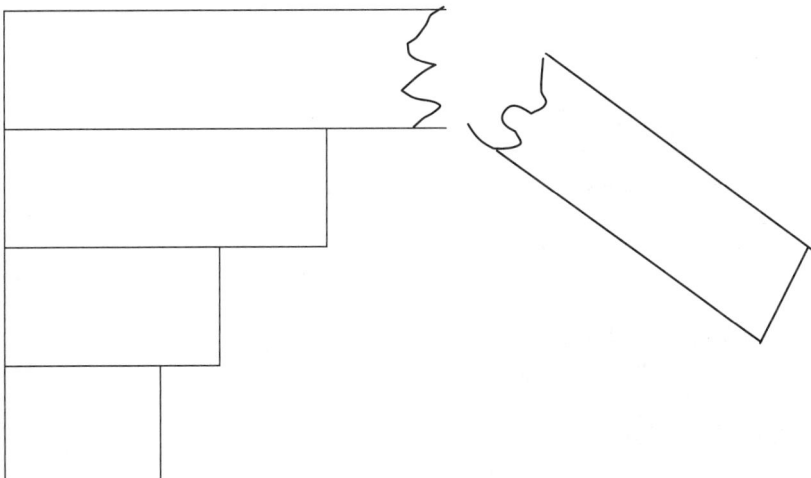

In most parishes, indeed most organizations of any kind, trust is an afterthought. We take note when it's missing. The blocks have tumbled over because we didn't pay attention to building the foundation. The idea that trust is something we can intentionally and successfully create is a new and foreign idea for many people.

The starting point

The starting point is to accept responsibility and begin. If the trust level is to improve, and a healthy community developed, we need new ways of listening and talking along with new ways of meeting and decision-making.

Listening & Talking

Building healthier communities requires a kind of talking often avoided in parishes. We live in the "safe-zone" where "all is comfortable" instead of the "better country" of deep acceptance and significant challenge where "all is well." Our communities can increase the conversations that involve self-disclosure and engage our mutual responsibility for this community of which we are members.

In *Community: The Structure of Belonging*,[49] Peter Block makes the case that one thing we can do to overcome the fragmentation of our communities is have different conversations than we usually have. He notes the conventional pattern we usually engage in— what he calls "just-talk."

His examples of "just-talk" include telling the story of how we got here, giving explanations and opinions, blaming and complaining, making reports and descriptions, seeking quick action.

These conversations can help us get connected to one another and allow us to understand something about our community. But they don't tend to produce an inclusion that is sustainable over time and under pressure or the kind of accountability and commitment needed for a healthy parish.

Block proposes a new set of conversations. The first two conversations are:

Invitation	This sets up the conversation. Whom do we want in this conversation? What is the conversation they are being invited to join? Is it about a "possibility?" Emphasize freedom of choice in their attending or not.
Possibility	Having conversation about how to bring into being a new thing. This conversation is about developing a description of the new reality that those who have gathered will set out to create. The starting point is not about problem solving and improving what is. It is not goals or a blue-sky vision.

I'll explore just the first conversation—invitation. This approach to "invitation" signals both the importance and genuineness about what will happen at the meeting. If you are invited, it's because someone believes you have something to bring to the discussion. There is some thought behind the invitation; it's not open to all comers. We want "you" to be with us. The invitation is also offered in a manner that asks the person to consider if they really want to be there. This approach to invitation sets things up for human connection and productivity.

But this approach also means violating the norms of politeness and inclusion common in many parishes. Some will feel excluded, even hurt, and it's important to understand the thinking behind the approach and its appropriate uses, including the extent of exclusion in any given situation. Different situations require different levels of inclusion, voice, and commitment. See additional information, below, in the section on Internal Commitment, Discernment and, especially Regular Community Meetings.

Using Block's method in beginning groups, whether for mutual spiritual guidance or a finance committee, means that those in the room are more likely to be ready for a significantly higher level of productivity and accountability than is often true in our parishes. Invitation and possibility are followed by the conversations of ownership, dissent including doubt, commitment, and gifts.

For Block, this is a process that has the effect of building community. Stephen Covey said, "Nothing is more exciting and bonding in relationships than creating together." It's important that we combine this with appreciation for what has already been created and is now part of parish life. Receive the tradition and innovate. Do both. Create new ways to engage the ancient. This is an emphasis on putting our energy into creating and shaping our life together.

Self-disclosure is another community building method involving talking and listening. Helene Oswald described two forms of self-disclosure[50] that she called personalness and openness. Her view was that both could increase trust. Each can be useful in establishing and maintaining relationships. It's a matter of emotional intelligence to understand each and know which best fits a particular situation or relationship.

Personalness is "revealing intimate, personal details of your private life." Openness is "revealing how you perceive and react to the present situation; sharing what you are feeling or thinking or wanting at that moment; telling another person how his/her behavior is affecting you."

Oswald continues:

> Some people mistake being personal for being open. They try to get emotionally close to another by making highly personal confessions about their lives. Sharing information about one's past may lead to a temporary feeling of intimacy, but a relationship is built by disclosing your reactions to events you both experience or to what the other person says or does.

A person comes to know you, not through your past history, but through encountering you in what you do and say in the present. Openness requires a willingness to risk rejection. However, being open also carries the potential for being recognized as authentic, for gaining respect, and for establishing a norm of integrity in the relationship. Being open with warm positive feelings and reactions communicates caring and affirmation. The other person(s) doesn't have to wonder about being heard or feeling supported.

Internal Commitment

The community's commitment to its own decisions is directly related to its health. The internal commitment of a critical mass of members to the parish's direction and culture is interdependent with a variety of other things—trust, collaboration, and the willingness of people to accept responsibility. All that is connected with the parish's ability to stay focused on its primary task of formation.

Commitment is built upon information and choice. The social scientist Chris Argyris developed a theory[51] that assumes we want as much internal commitment as possible in an organization. The more people have such an ownership of the decisions made, the direction we are going in, the more it will be sustainable and survive under pressure. When there is internal commitment it's more likely that people will have energy for it and act to implement the decision.

Leaders develop such commitment not by exhortation and pressure but through attention to the decision making process. The more people get engaged with information about an issue (ideas, feelings, research), the more equipped they are to see the options available and make informed decisions. The more they are making decisions based on a free choice, rather than from coercion or habit, the greater the likelihood they will have the commitment necessary to follow through.

Obviously it's not possible for the whole community to be involved in all the decisions any parish needs to make. The priest, vestry, or those with designated authority need to make the routine decisions that keep a parish working. Leaders also need to accept responsibility to act in situations of crisis when timely action is essential. On occasion leaders also will need to be the emotional circuit breakers when the community is extremely anxious. This is the legitimate case for hierarchy in any organization or community.

Argyris's theory isn't a case for having the whole community involved in any particular decision. It's simply to say that, to the extent people are involved, the information they are working with is valid and useful, and they have real choices before them, the likelihood of ending up with strong internal commitment is increased.

Discernment

Discernment has become a frequently misused concept in the church. Some clergy and parishes get carried away thinking that all decision-making is discernment. One parish was going to discern what kind of copier to purchase, as though God had a particular brand and model in mind.

One way of thinking about discernment processes in the community is that they have to do with decisions requiring us to see what's not obvious; maybe to be able to see "whatever is true, whatever is honorable, whatever is just, whatever is pure, whatever is pleasing, and whatever is commendable." (Philippians 4:8). Discernment suggests the desire and ability to look beyond what is apparent, to use our capacity for reflection, empathy and practical judgment so we might see clearly.

Discernment and decision-making are interrelated processes. The parish needs valid and useful information, clarity about its choices, freedom from coercion and destructive repetitive patterns, and emotional maturity in its leadership. We also need an understanding of the spiritual life, ways of being reflective, and a functional spiritual discipline.

It is a destructive and mistaken assumption to think that God has one right answer or path for us and we are to "discern" it. It's a misguided view to think of discernment as "uncovering" what God wills for us. Real discernment is an engagement with God, at times a wrestling with God, leading us to holiness as a community and as individuals.

Discernment is collaboration with God in shaping our common life. Thomas Merton expressed it this way, "Our vocation is not simply to be, but to work together with God in the creation of our own life, our own identity, our own destiny—to work out our own identity in God, which the Bible calls 'working out salvation,' is a labor which requires sacrifice and anguish, risk and many tears."

Communal discernment is the process by which a community of faith seeks to see God's movement in the world and in that community's life. It is our attempt to see "rightly;" to see our experience and our goals through the eyes of Christ. It is our striving to listen deeply and grow in our conformity with God's love for us.

There may be many faithful pathways for a parish or an individual. Discernment isn't about finding the one right way. It is about grounding our life in prayer, reflectiveness, and community. It is also about testing the spirit of our decisions: can we see the Spirit's movement, the influence of the church and a consistency with history and gifts?

Communal discernment is already happening in all Christian communities. It may be more or less skilled, grounded or intentional in various communities. To the extent a community is grounded in Eucharist and the daily prayers, and has ways of being reflective, that will show itself in the decisions made and the life lived.

In any case, our discernment is only confirmed over time. It is confirmed by the experience and acceptance of the community.

The measure is whether the decision brought us to holiness rather than whether the decision was "correct."

Regular community meetings

The parish community needs regular meetings over the course of the year. At times the whole parish, at other times a congregation within the parish. That will depend on the issues to be engaged. These meetings need to make use of the methods known to facilitate dialogue and listening. Having three or four such meetings each year provides the opportunity to engage more people in the significant questions of the community's life.

It is important that these not turn into "town meetings" with their image of a contentious and argumentative spirit. It's also important that they not undercut the responsibility of the rector and vestry for decisions they have to make. They are a chance for leaders to test things with the community and for the community to hear its own voice. The effect of such regular gatherings is usually increased trust and commitment.

Wait for all to arrive

You may recall the 2010 experience of the 33 miners in Chile. There had been a cave-in on August 5. For 17 days no one above ground knew if the miners were alive. Engineers drilling in search finally found them. They were underground for 69 days and they all survived.

In their time in the mine they developed a working community that included smaller groupings of eleven, and involved prayer and an interesting norm around meals. As of early September the hole through which all materials, food and messages had to pass was just 4 inches across. Luis Urzua, the shift leader, insisted that all the miners wait until everyone got food through the borehole before anyone began to eat. [52]

This is an act of community that we see in First Corinthians, 11:33 ("when you come together to eat, wait for one another") and Benedict's Rule. Benedict wanted all to gather for the meal so they could all "pray together and sit down to table at the same time."

In the same chapter of the Rule a similar expectation is applied to the Office. Along with that expectation comes one about personal responsibility.

As soon as the signal for the time of the divine office is heard, let everyone, leaving whatever he hath in his hands, hasten with all speed, yet with gravity, that there may be no cause for levity. Therefore, let nothing be preferred to the Work of God.

Rule of St. Benedict, Chapter XLIII

A parish can engage several related spiritual practices that can build up the community.

- Arrange meals in a way that easily allows all to begin eating at the same time.

- Wait for all to arrive before beginning a meeting. When a person needs to leave the room, suspend the discussion until all are together again.

- Don't have any other activities taking place at the times of Eucharist and Office. The parish business office can take a break and meetings can begin after the times of worship.

Around the circle

This is a useful method of allowing everyone to be heard, and is something I've used with up to 45 people. Participants speak in turn around the circle. The comment is to be brief and on one point. The method helps equalize the voices in the room so the more hesitant are heard along with the more assertive. It can be especially useful when dealing with controversial issues.

Variations include the fishbowl and the Samoan circle. The methods are defined in different ways by various facilitators. In both cases there is a group that sits within the larger circle of participants and engages in a conversation. The inner group is to consist of the various positions on an issue, or might be an "expert panel."

Depending on your objectives and issues, such as the time available, the outer group might remain silent, or there might be an opportunity for comment or questions from the outer circle, or there might be a way for someone from the outer circle to join the inner circle.

Testing [53]

In a testing process an issue is identified and a spectrum, scale, is created to reflect the views present in the community. For example:

We need to do less of this	We need to stay with the current amount	We need to do more of this

The "testing process" can be done for a few minutes at coffee hour, at vestry meetings, in working teams and at parish community meetings. It will usually be most effective if done when the group is gathered and can respond and discuss the result, formally or informally.

Face-to-face processes are usually more effective in promoting careful listening and effective response. A rule of thumb might be to use a "testing process" about four times per year with the whole community and possibly ten times with the vestry.

The testing process is a way to find out where the larger community stands on certain questions or issues. It helps both the community and the leadership get a sense of where the group is collectively. It's important for parish leaders and the congregation to understand that the testing process is *not* a way to shift decision-making authority to a vote of the congregation. The results do not mean that any particular change will take place.

Examples of useful areas to test: satisfaction with the amount of silence in liturgy; sense of understanding and competence with using the Daily Office; satisfaction with existing methods of Reflection; overall satisfaction with parish life.

Examples of ways of framing questions or the discussion that are *not* useful include setting up binary responses, such as, "I would prefer piano music to the organ at 10:30." Similarly, you don't want to test in areas where the group is not competent to respond.

Context matters. It might, for instance, be very useful for the rector to gather specific feedback about liturgical issues or her sermons from a small, trusted group of parishioners who know something about liturgy and about homiletics. This would not, however, be a useful exercise if expanded to the parish as a whole.

Arrangement of space

Peter Block maintains that in arranging meeting space we are trying "to build relatedness, accountability, and commitment." "Physical space is more decisive in creating community than we realize. Most meeting spaces are designed for control, negotiation, and persuasion...Community is built when we sit in circles, when there are windows and the walls have signs of life, when every voice can be equally heard." Block prefers that there be no tables.[54]

Circles provide a sense of closeness, allow people to better notice body language, and invite people to lean in toward one another. When the work involves processes such as brainstorming, group problem solving or strategizing, or the use of a method such as force field analysis or SWOT, the circle can be opened at an end to allow the use of newsprint pads for recording the work. In those cases the objective is to maximize the ability of people to see one another and the workspace with the newsprint pads.

Use of newsprint (flip chart pads)

Using newsprint pads to record the group's thinking can improve participation, reduce repetition, and help people feel heard.

The best arrangement is to have pegs in a wall allowing several pads to be hung. It's better use of space, reduces the number of flip chart easels a parish needs, and eliminates the temptation to "flip" the page over and thus hide the work just completed.

Reflection & Community: Integration

Rising from the "ground" of Eucharist and Daily Office are two activities that serve to integrate life: reflection and community. The weekly practice of Eucharist, along with the daily practice of Office, familiarize us with the ways of heaven. Abraham Heschel saw worship as "a way of seeing the world in the light of God."

Community and reflection are part of what makes life whole. What we have become acclimated to in worship, the habits of good liturgy (listening, engagement, patience, and so on), shape our contemplation and are enfleshed in our life with others.

The end of all things is near; therefore be serious and discipline yourselves for the sake of your prayers. Above all, maintain constant love for one another, for love covers a multitude of sins. Be hospitable to one another without complaining. Like good stewards of the manifold grace of God, serve one another with whatever gift each of you has received. Whoever speaks must do so as one speaking the very words of God; whoever serves must do so with the strength that God supplies, so that God may be glorified in all things through Jesus Christ. To him belong the glory and the power forever and ever. Amen.

1 Peter 4: 7 – 11

Six

Service

Serve one another

Serving one another comes naturally in a healthy parish. It happens in quiet and unacknowledged ways week by week. We ask after one another, "Have you finished the radiation treatments?" "How is your son doing at school?" We attend the funeral of a member's mother. At coffee hour we bring coffee and cake to those with mobility problems. There are tender and kind actions, a hand briefly on a shoulder, a smile in greeting, stopping to listen.

Serve the world

"Out of the believer's heart shall flow rivers of living water." (John 7:38) This is possible because the Spirit has been given to us as a guarantee or promise of what is to come. (2 Cor. 5:5) This is what Martin Thornton was getting at in his book *Spiritual Direction*:

> *Aquinas got it right: prayer is 'loving God in act so that the divine life can communicate itself to us and through us to the world.' Christian action is not action of which Jesus approves but action that he performs through his incorporated, and therefore prayerful, disciples.*

Service in Daily Life

The primary service of the baptized person is in the routines and places of daily life. We serve in our friendships, family, work and civic life.

Mark Gibbs was a significant voice throughout the 1970s in the lay ministry movement. He saw three categories of ministers. There were the professional clergy, making up around 1% of the total. About 10% he called "churchly" laity. These were the people with gifts offered primarily within the institutional church and absolutely necessary for the well being of the church.

Then there were the 89% whom Gibbs called the "secular laity." Some were deeply involved in the parish church, others less so. But according to Gibbs they "do wish to serve God faithfully in one way or another; they will not do this primarily in church organizations, but in the other secular structures of their lives."[55] Of course, even for the ten percent he thought of as "churchly Christians" most of their service was in the daily stuff of family, friendship, civic life, and workplace.

Influence institutions effectively from within

Our service is also about how we use our influence and power. It was Pope John XXIII who in *Pacem in Terris* wrote of the lay apostolate:

It is vitally necessary for them to endeavor, in the light of Christian faith and with love as their guide, to ensure that every institution whether economic, social, cultural or political, be such as not to obstruct but rather to facilitate man's self betterment, both in the natural and in the supernatural order. And yet, if they are to imbue civilization with right ideals and Christian principles, it is not enough for our sons to be illumined by the heavenly light of faith and to be fired with enthusiasm for a cause; they must involve themselves in the work of these institutions, and strive to influence them effectively from within.

All too often the official bodies of the church talk as though the church is outside other institutions and must make its voice heard from that external position. Bishops and clergy may speak in a manner suggesting that the leaders of secular institutions are people with a lack of concern for peace, justice, and the humane treatment of people.

Of course in one sense the church is an institution alongside other institutions. It has every right to address the others.

However, we might do that with more awareness of our own sins and limitations. A bit of humility may be good for us and also help us be heard.

Pope John's message was placing the emphasis on another reality. *The church is already present in all the institutions.* The baptized are the leaders and workers in many of those institutions. Christian influence is already happening.

William Temple, one-time Archbishop of Canterbury, had 20 years earlier pointed in the same direction, "Nine-tenths of the work of the Church in the world is done by Christian people fulfilling responsibilities and performing tasks which in themselves are not part of the official system of the Church at all." In a later work, Temple wrote of the organic reality of the Body, "the stream of redemptive power flows out from the church through the lives of its members into the society which they influence."[56]

In the routines of daily life

We diminish our understanding of service if it's focused only on the poor or about our volunteer time or some great cause. Most of the ways in which we serve come in the routines of daily life.

Ed Silva was the musician at St. Elisabeth's in South Philadelphia. Ed once explained to me his spiritual practice around homeless people asking for money. He said something like this: "I decided to just give the person money. I know that much of the time I'm being scammed. I know that there's a case to be made to only give money through organizations. Thinking about all that wasn't doing my soul much good. I just needed to give the money."

I went in a different direction from Ed. I decided I didn't want to hand out money on the street, even though I frequently feel guilty in refusing. I selected two Seattle groups to give a donation to each month. It's on my schedule, so I do it.

Ted Kennedy, Jr., told this story at his father's burial mass. "I once told him that he had accidentally left some money—I remember this when I was a little kid—on the sink in our hotel room. And he replied, 'Teddy, let me tell you something, making beds all day is back breaking work. The woman who has to clean up after us today has a family to feed.' " That story has changed my

111

practice in hotels. I travel frequently in my consulting practice. That means a lot of hotel time. From now on I'll be leaving money.

I generally make it a practice to use UPS or the postal service instead of Fed Ex because I believe I have a moral obligation to support businesses that are unionized. I buy most of my groceries at a co-op because it's both unionized and a co-op. I get my health services from Group Health, another co-op.

We can all integrate small practices of generosity and justice into our daily routines. Along with that we might maintain the practice of not driving others crazy with how they should do what we do.

Service within the parish

Our service to one another in the parish is mostly by way of the informal exchanges, the small kindnesses, and the occasional run-ins. Much of our service is connected to being part of a parish community and being in relationship with others. We grow up thorough those encounters. We serve one another in those encounters.

Some will serve in more institutional ways, such as on vestries, teaching, and maintaining the property. We will give something of our life, that gift of God, to something other than ourselves. The service matters because the parish needs it but even more, those who offer it have a need to offer it. It is an aspect of their vocation, of who they are in Christ. In serving they step beyond themselves and become something better.

These forms of service are opportunities for self-awareness and therefore personal and spiritual growth. I am invited to serve the Body of Christ, the People of God. I may also be tempted to claim and protect turf, to accumulate power and to puff myself up. Parishes are healthier when there are opportunities to assess and talk about all this.

The priest's oversight and pastoral role is largely about guiding the diversity of gifts and ministries so they might be expressed in harmony. It's seen in microcosm as the priest presides at the Eucharist and meetings of the community and vestry.

112

Service through the parish

Most parishes have some form of collective service ministry. Members with a vocational inclination toward serving the poor, the marginalized and the oppressed carry out these service ministries in the name of the whole parish.

In some parishes this is a formally authorized parish activity. Other parishes take the stance of allowing anyone to launch a service ministry within broad guidelines. The guidelines may include: the activity is consistent with the values of this parish, doesn't request budget support, invites member participation (time, money, prayer) in ways provided in this parish.

One caution: There are parishes where those engaged in service ministries take on a self-righteous tone toward the whole parish community. The diversity of gifts and callings in the Body of Christ is negated by pressure for everyone to participate in a particular ministry.

A parish may also have an impact as an institution by how it invests its funds, uses its purchasing power, and educates its members in civic responsibility.

Reject the "guilting" machine

Segments of the church continue to approach service by way of guilt—if we can make people feel bad enough maybe they'll do what we think they should do. It finds expression in some parish churches where a few members attempt to "guilt" the rest over their lack of greenness, failure to treat the homeless "properly," or not giving enough time to parish service projects. It reaches its high point around Christmas as the pleasure of the secular feast is assaulted in the name of a purer feast. Or the impulse to spend more on gifts for those we love is set over against the needs of the poor.

The alternative is to join Underhill in trusting that we and all people were created for service (also for awe and adoration). It's in our make up. The parish can either nurture and strengthen us based on that assumption or attempt to "guilt" us based on a less orthodox set of assumptions.

The parish can

- Hold in front of its members the moral vision of Christian Faith.[57]

- Stress that the primary place, and possibly most effective place, of service for the Christian is in daily life. We serve within our friendships, families, work, and civic life.

- Provide settings in which members identify how they serve, how they may better serve, and the gifts each brings to that task. Offer materials and processes that include daily life and the routine habits of life in developing a spiritual discipline.

- Avoid a kind of institutionalism that undervalues the primary service of members. Too many web sites omit any mention of the daily life ministries of members and instead focus on what can be done in and through the parish.

- Ground service in the other spiritual practices

Grounded in adoration and awe

Evelyn Underhill pointed to the need for service to be built upon prayer and a stance toward life in which, "one's first duty is adoration, and one's second duty is awe and only one's third duty is service. And that for those three things and nothing else, addressed to God and no one else, you and I and all other countless human creatures evolved upon the surface of this planet were created. We observe then that two of the three things for which our souls were made are matters of attitude, of relation: adoration and awe. Unless these two are right, the last of the triad, service, won't be right. Unless the whole of your... life is a movement of praise and adoration, unless it is instinct with awe, the work which the life produces won't be much good."[58]

Service is first a stance, an attitude, influencing and filling all our activities. We assume that God strengthens our "hearts in holiness." (1 Thessalonians 3:13)

The parish can reinforce that stance in many ways:

- Maintain a deep and rich life of worship and prayer as a

community.

- On occasion have parish service activities include times of worship and reflection. As the feeding program begins the day, have volunteers gather for Morning Prayer. In training programs related to service projects include individual and group reflection—What draws you to this work? Where is the presence of Jesus Christ in the people, things and circumstances of this work?

- Close the parish office when the Eucharist is being celebrated or the Office said.

It's organic to the Body of Christ

Our tradition has stressed the organic nature of Christian action and service. Temple wrote of this organic reality, "the stream of redemptive power flows out from the church through the lives of its members into the society which they influence."[59]

The same point was made by James Otis Sargent Huntington, OHC. "Holiness is the brightness of divine love, and love is never idle; it must accomplish great things. Love must act as light must shine and fire must burn."

I believe that part of how this works is through empathy. "Empathy is the process of placing oneself in the frame of reference of another, perceiving the world as the other perceives it, sharing his or her world imaginatively. Incarnation means that God assumes our frame of reference, entering into our human situation of finitude and estrangement, sharing our human condition even unto death."[60]   There is a movement from empathy to intercession to service.

Empathy is a form of acceptance. In the quote above, Thomas Oden suggests that such acceptance points beyond itself to God's acceptance of the person. This is an essential human competence. None of us will get it perfectly right but we can desire it and work at increasing our capacity for it.

Narcissism is one stance that blocks empathy. Anther more common barrier is our fear that if we are empathetic we will lose ourselves; that we will give up something important about ourselves or that we will not fulfill the responsibilities of the role we are in at the time. I've heard bishops and rectors speak against being empathetic in situations where they may need to make decisions negatively impacting a person's life. They fear that being empathetic will paralyze them.

Passion

Lyndon Johnson's success at gaining Medicare for the American people was possible because of many factors: the time was right and his political skills were extraordinary. Another major element was his passion for that cause. It was a service to which he had a deep commitment.

In a conversation with Vice President Hubert Humphrey he said, "Don't ever argue with me [about health]. I'll go a hundred million or a billion on health or education. I don't argue about that any more than I argue about Lady Bird [Mrs. Johnson] buying flour. You got to have flour and coffee in your house. Education and health. I'll spend the goddamn money. I may cut back some tanks. But not on health."[61]

In my own work, what I've seen is that congregational development is effective when there's a diocesan staff person with passion for it; it is effective when the rector has enthusiasm for it.

Find a way to serve that calls on your passion. Harness that passion with perseverance and self-knowledge.

In our dying

Even at the end there is service. Harry Patch was Britain's last World War I veteran, dying at age 111 in 2009. He had served as a machine gunner on the Western Front. After turning 100 he began to speak of his experience and his reflection on that experience. War, he said, was "the calculated and condoned slaughter of human beings."

He wanted those on both sides of the war to be honored and mourned. "Irrespective of the uniforms we wore, we were all victims." At the 90th anniversary remembrance services of the armistice ending the war, he said, "Remember the Germans." At his funeral two German soldiers in full dress uniform were honorary pallbearers, and a German diplomat read from Paul on reconciliation. Soldiers from his old regiment carried the casket and there were no weapons permitted in Wells Cathedral.[62]

The parish can help people serve in their dying. For most, death will not provide the level of opportunity to serve seen in Harry Patch's funeral. So, we may focus on the simpler acts: prepare a will, provide end of life instructions, make it easy for people to find important papers, if possible leave something to serve the common good and something to your parish, and consider how you will say goodbye if circumstances allow. And as with Harry Patch, we can seek reconciliation at the end. The parish can provide forms, legal clinics, guidance, and the sacraments.

Benedict invited his monks to meditate on death. Phil Ochs sang, "So I guess I'll have to do it while I'm here." I believe both were getting at the same thing. While we live we can enjoy our life together in community, we can love and be loved, we can participate in "dances of delight," and "do our share."[63]

A wise and generous love

In singing Newman's "Praise to the Holiest in the height" we give thanks for God's wise and generous love. A wise love that did strive and prevail in Christ; a generous love to see us through the suffering and death we share in Christ.

That's the way of Christian action—wisdom and generosity. A generosity that offers service from an enlarged and kind heart. A wisdom that serves with good sense and insight.

Most of us are inclined toward one or the other. Generosity that stands alone may easily become sentimental and offer help that does damage, that is more about our need than those we would serve. Wisdom standing alone can be cold in how right it is and driven by our fears of those we would serve.

In Christ the two are held together. And by our baptism we are in Christ and Christ is in us. We are capable of generosity and wisdom; we can learn to approach our service that way.

Service: Action

Martin Thornton's quote from the beginning of this chapter expresses the connection among action and the grounding practices of Eucharist and Office, and the integrating practices of reflection and community. Here it is again: "Aquinas got it right: prayer is 'loving God in act so that the divine life can communicate itself to us and through us to the world.' Christian action is not action of which Jesus approves but action that he performs through his incorporated, and therefore prayerful, disciples."

We would rather be ruined than changed,
We would rather die in our dread
Than climb the cross of the moment
And let our illusions die.

W. H. Auden

Seven

The Process of Change

Two assertions and two related questions:

1. **The primary task of the parish church is to form Christians.**

   The gifts of the church are "to equip the saints for the work of ministry, for building up the body of Christ, until all of us come to the unity of the faith and of the knowledge of the Son of God, to maturity, to the measure of the full stature of Christ." (Ephesians 4.12-13)

2. **How can the parish be a place that helps that happen?**

   The parish can help in the development of Christian character by offering direction, methods, and an understanding of how virtue and productive spiritual practices become habitual.

3. **We are to build Christian proficiency.**

   It's not a new idea. Aristotle said, "Excellence is an art won by training and habituation. We do not act rightly because we have virtue or excellence, but we rather have those because we have acted rightly. We are what we repeatedly do. Excellence, then, is not an act but a habit."

   In part, Christian proficiency and formation is also developed through intentional training, guiding, and coaching. The parish can assist its members become more competent for participation in the Eucharist and Daily Office, sharing in the common life of a community, engaging in reflection, and offering service in the places they find themselves.

4. **How can we shape such a parish?**

   I'll address that in the remainder of this chapter and point the reader to my earlier books: *Fill All Things: The Dynamics of Spirituality in the Parish Church* and *Power from on High: A Model for Parish Life and Development.*

Shaping a healthy community

I'm going to highlight just a few considerations about the process of change:

- Understand and use a critical mass strategy.

- Begin with what's easy to do.

- Understand what's involved in the "Use of Self".

- Understand the behaviors and assumptions that are barriers to change.

- Parish clergy engage parishioners around their spiritual life

- Place the parish in a context of support, competency building, and accountability

Understand and use a critical mass strategy

Critical mass theories are about building the level of commitment, competence and emotional maturity at the center of the organization so that it grounds the system in a mission orientation and an organizational culture that supports the mission. This will take the shape of a series of circles, one within the other. Those at the center will share more of the "common language" of healthy and useful skills, knowledge, attitudes and values.

Critical mass models invite leaders to attend to building the center and to stop the tendency to obsess about "fixing" the problems and dysfunction at the edges. New and unskilled leaders are especially inclined to focus on the "difficult people" or those who constantly demand personal attention, or the crisis of the moment.

A critical mass model suggests that we should give much more of our time and energy to developing the center. Support and build the capacity of those willing and able to more fully give themselves, whether to the overall health of the parish or to a particular project that moves toward health.

The emerging field of network science may help us understand how a critical mass develops. Network science studies how behavioral changes spread through social systems. There's an obvious link to developing and spreading emotional intelligence, sound spiritual practice, and virtues such as kindness, patience, gentleness, courage and perseverance.

These social networks are of people in face-to-face contact, people we see regularly. Researchers are looking at how the structure of these networks affects our adopting and sustaining habits. There's some evidence that networks of overlapping social ties were the most effective. That is to say, we don't know everyone in the network, but we know some people and they know others. It's like a web. In such networks, people catch things from one another.

"Most of us are already aware of the direct effect we have on our friends and family; our actions can make them happy or sad, healthy or sick, even rich or poor. But we rarely consider that everything we think, feel, do or say can spread far beyond the people we know...As part of a social network, we transcend ourselves, for good or ill, and become part of something much larger. We are connected." [64]

Parish leaders don't control the social networks that exist within and beyond the parish. But they can encourage social connections and look favorably upon friendships in the parish. They may also influence those networks through the overall culture, climate, structures and processes of the parish. Exercising such influence has the capacity to build a critical mass around healthy and faithful practices.

Malcolm Gladwell's concept of the tipping point[65] is related to the idea of critical mass. A tipping point is when the impetus for change becomes unstoppable. Gladwell defines a tipping point as "the moment of critical mass, the threshold, the boiling point."

Gladwell believes, "Ideas and products and messages and behaviors spread like viruses do." To facilitate critical mass around a healthier set of parish habits we might pay attention to Gladwell's notion that three types of people are needed: 1) connectors, those who easily make friends and build connections; 2) people with the new and needed competencies such as spiritual practice and emotional intelligence; and 3) people with skills at persuading and negotiating. Not much good will happen in a parish if leaders discourage social connection, and/or are unskilled in the spiritual life, and/or are not able to draw members toward healthier practice.

The Shape of the Parish model is an example of a critical mass approach. See the Resources section for more on the model.

The Shape of the Parish model assumes that developing a "critical mass" around spiritual life and practice has the effect of drawing more people, and the parish as a whole, into a deeper relationship with God and the church. The existence of a critical mass of Apostolic Faith people in a parish can orient the parish toward Christ and away from its preoccupation with the more trivial aspects of religion and parish life.

By their behavior and character those closer to the center contribute to establishing a climate, "an energy not their own," that attracts others toward the center. By living the faith they draw others deeper into God. They become a means of grace for the parish by their contagious influence.

A goal might be to develop a critical mass of people of Apostolic Faith in the parish making up 15—20% of Sunday attendees. That would, in most situations, provide the weight needed to orient the parish in a healthy direction. What's needed is a condition where those of Apostolic Faith and Practice constitute a critical mass, where there are enough of them that they are setting the tone and climate.

In addition, leaders need to facilitate and strengthen the critical mass, the Apostolic core, by firmly and gently tilting the structures, processes and climate of the parish toward maturity and health. The whole atmosphere of the parish says that there is more; more than we have yet experienced and known.

The grounding of the parish in health and faithfulness then is enfleshed; made real in the lives of men and women. It is in the habits of people, not just the statements of leaders.

There are several interrelated areas in which special attention might have rewards in building critical mass:

- Use a Foundations Course[66] approach in creating a critical mass of members who have some competence for living the life.

- The competent participation of a critical mass of the congregation in the Eucharist.

- The development of common spiritual practices in the congregation around Eucharist, the Daily Prayers of the Church, reflection, community and service.

- Understanding and using the system dynamics of the parish's spiritual life. For example, knowing that the parish's Eucharist is deepened and enriched by the presence of a critical mass of members who join in the Daily Office and some form of personal devotions during the week.

Using Shape of the Parish as a starting point, there are three broad objectives that make up a critical mass strategy.

1. Nurture the Shape. If there are no people of Apostolic Faith, seek ways to establish a core of such people in the parish community; if there is no Vicarious ring, build relationships with other communities of people. Assume that it will take years to do these things.

2. Accept and Invite. Take a stance in which you *accept* people wherever they are in the journey and *invite* them to go deeper. Include people in a manner that respects and loves them for who they are now while also seeking opportunities to offer new ways and new life.

3. Set Loose the Dynamic. Root the overall climate of the parish in Apostolic Faith and set loose the dynamic by building the appropriate culture.

Begin with what's easy to do

Start in places that are both strategic and "easy." That could include working with groups of people of apostolic faith in mutual spiritual guidance and exploring their vocation in the family, workplace and civic life; begin and maintain an adult foundations course; train the congregation for participation in the Eucharist; begin using the Daily Office during the week. Work with promising areas—begin in the places of health, strength and success.

Develop initiatives or interventions unlikely to cause much resistance. Consider:

- An activity people don't *have to* participate in. Change the Liturgy on Sunday and it impacts everyone and is likely to produce more resistance. Offer Evening Prayer every weeknight and it overtly affects only those who want to attend. Over time, the saying of the Office will influence the Sunday Eucharist.

- Activities that don't require a critical mass of support or high levels of internal commitment to get started.

- Things that are within the priest's assumed scope of initiation—adult education, mid-week worship, spiritual development. Clergy who have given lay committees the impression that they control such areas have made a serious mistake. It's fine to include people in these areas as long as that doesn't create a bottleneck.

Examples of such initiatives or interventions:

- Offering Foundations Courses.

- Anglican Spirituality: Spiritual Practice in Our Tradition— a six session program using experiential methods to teach people spiritual practices based on the model of this book. This could also be a module within a Foundations Course.

- Equipping individuals to be able to use the Office.

- Public saying of the Office—organizing a group of people to say it at least four times a week.

- Eucharistic Spirituality—two or three sessions each year, each about an hour to an hour-and-a-half, on practices of the person in the pew.

There are many others that may or may not cause resistance. A few examples:

126

- Establish listening processes in the parish (see the chapter on Community in this book, the section on "Theory and Methods" and *Fill All Things* pages 107—115).

- Improve the Sunday experience. Create a Sunday morning experience that is focused on the gathering of the Eucharistic community. Work at having a great Liturgy and social time together. Make it an event that centers and renews, rather than simply another source of demands and pressure for their time, money, and energy. Develop a community that is competent for Eucharistic worship, spirituality and living.

- Improve vestry meetings by engaging self-assessment processes and making use of the methods mentioned in the chapter on Community.

Paying attention to readiness will help identify the "easy" initiatives in a particular parish. What is this parish ready to do? If there isn't a readiness to proceed with an improvement, for example listening processes, we need to ask, "What can we do to build that readiness?"

For example, with listening processes it is usually helpful to start with equipping people with the related skills, knowledge and methods. One of the reasons people resist new ways is that they fear appearing incompetent. The question then becomes, how do I introduce new competencies without doing that in the established groups, such as the vestry? One possibility is to offer a program in effective small groups that trains people in basic facilitation skills such as using newsprint, communication skills, and how to avoid screening the ideas of others.

Or, as part of the Foundations Course, have a module on Benedictine Spirituality that explores the spirituality of listening while teaching people ways to focus on the speaker and how to take a stance that assumes God may have a word for us in the words of others. Skills such as these also can be connected with our behavior during the Liturgy.

Another possible action is identifying settings where you can introduce the listening skills and processes without generating

127

resistance. There's often more leeway in a foundations course, an orientation of new members, the vestry retreat, and special parish community meetings. You may also find it easier to introduce listening methods in groups you know to be more receptive. An external consultant may be able to help people try new ways that would generate opposition if offered by the parish's leadership.

Once the new skills and methods have been introduced here and there, it may be easier to bring them into the vestry or other group. In fact, some people will wonder why it took you so long to do it.

Another aspect of starting in easy places is to think about the development of the parish in terms of at least three to five years. It will take that kind of time to significantly improve the community and organizational life of the congregation so it is "owned" and sustainable. Watch out for attempts at a quick fix. The quick fix compulsion only adds to the stress and encourages a kind of illusion about what it takes to change a parish.

If you are clear about the revitalization effort being both immediate and long term, you can accept a mindset of one initiative after another. Assume you will do dozens of interventions each year. Think of your work as moving from one congregational development initiative to another, and over the years shaping a healthier parish.

There's a good bit of repetitiveness involved. You offer the Eucharistic practices program three times a year, year after year. It never ends because there are always new people joining and older members wanting a refresher experience. Over time you build a competent Eucharistic community—10 people at the June session, six in the fall session. In time there's a critical mass and things are different.

This is a process of nurturing what organization development practitioners call "common language." You want to nurture a "common language" of spiritual practice. It helps to use a map such as that provided in this book: Eucharist and Office, Reflection and Community, and Service.

Have some clarity about the skills, knowledge, attitudes and values that will be taught in relationship to the map. Teach, train, and coach. Remember that by doing this, you are providing options and choices about a deeper spiritual life, not ordering parishioners to do it your way.

Use of Self

The presiding priest of the community needs to establish habits and skills that help her or him be a centered and healthy presence as leader of the community in its life and worship. This certainly means being part of those who share the "common language." The priest needs to engage the map—Eucharist and Office, Community and Reflection, and Service.

It also means accepting oneself as a person on a journey to wholeness and holiness. We need to assume that we need to be changed. This is true for all parish leaders, but especially so for the clergy.

The other "use of self" issue is for all leaders to attend to their own emotional and social intelligence. This includes expanding and increasing our capacity for: connection with others, authenticity, self-awareness and self-management, the ability to read the dynamics in situations and to act effectively in the situation.

This involves accepting responsibility for the choices we make, including when we don't see choices. Part of our work is to expand the range of choices we see rather than be stuck on "automatic pilot."

We can help ourselves by establishing appropriate feedback processes about our leadership and receiving help from a spiritual director or therapist in seeing how our beliefs and mental models influence our thinking and the choices we see. There are what is called reframing[67] methods that can help us expand our understanding and sense of what is possible in a particular situation.

Both emotional intelligence and spiritual practice abilities are addressed in a program such as Shaping the Parish™. The lab training approach of LTI (Leadership Training Institute) and NTL

(National Training Labs) is especially useful in addressing emotional intelligence.

Understand the behaviors and assumptions that are barriers to change

It can be useful to acknowledge how we get in our own way, shoot ourselves in the foot, and block needed changes. This is an act of humility. We may acknowledge that what we are currently doing isn't working, even that we don't know what to do about it. That gives us a place to start. Then we may find ourselves free to receive help around our spiritual life, emotional and social intelligence, and the methods and tools of change.

A Distorting Influence: Well-Meaning Worriers

I was early for the Eucharist. Very early. I sat in the pew and did a perfunctory, though still useful, *lectio* on a reading for the day. Then my mind drifted back to a dynamic I'd seen in several parishes. It had to do with changes, large and small, that had been blocked by fear. I was groping for a word or phase to capture the dynamic. A word or phrase I could use in this section of the book. The Mass began and I let it go.

Later I settled in with eggs, toast and the *New York Times*. Nicholas Kristof was writing about America's history of fear around people who were new and unfamiliar. In regard to the latest manifestation of fear he wrote, "Most of the opponents aren't bigots but well-meaning worriers."[68] That was the phrase I wanted!

"Well-meaning worriers" captured it for me. Much of what undercut needed changes in parishes wasn't outright opposition. It was someone worrying about some hypothetical, or sometimes real, person or group whose feelings would be hurt or who would misunderstand or who would be offended.

"Well-meaning worriers" would plug into a poorly-differentiated rector or warden and the rector or warden would "catch" the worry. The worriers didn't themselves feel hurt or offended. They were just worried that someone might feel that way.

Pray for love.

Conversations we can't or don't know how to have

All too often we can't have the kind of conversations we need to have if change is to occur. We pontificate, we repeat the same positions endlessly, we think about what we're going to say next instead of listening to the person speaking, we try to build trust by telling our stories instead of being open about our feelings, we blame and grumble, and we fill our time at meetings with making reports.

"Undiscussables" are conversations we don't know how to have. We are certain that if we begin such a conversation someone will die. Well maybe not really die but someone will get badly hurt. The stance is that this is the way things are and there is nothing that can be done about it.

How we handle "undiscussables" is key in our ability to facilitate needed change.

We need conversations about creating the things we long for, the things that make for health and salvation. We need conversations in which we connect to one another and become a community.

It's not so much that we don't want such conversations. We may be stuck in the ways we know; we may lack the skills, discipline or courage to behave differently.

Pray for courage.

Another Distorting Influence: False and Limited Analogies[69]

Most people in any parish have a limited grasp of the nature and mission of the church. The tradition's language of People of God and Body of Christ may be accepted with little sense of what flows from such images.

People do want to make sense of their parish community. They often have an investment in finding a way of describing the parish and in doing that, making a kind of meaning. So, we draw on images and analogies from other spheres of life. We take what is familiar to us, what makes sense to us, and we apply it to the church. Parishioners are also members of clubs, work in a business, are part of families, may be involved in a political or

131

social change movement, and give time or money to various social service groups. The purposes and ways of those other groups are frequently used in an attempt to understand the parish church.

In that process things get distorted. Vestries become boards of directors and rectors CEOs or executive directors. There's talk of how the parish needs to be run more like a business. Or stewardship is reduced to pledging and pledging in turn is reduced to "dues" or a kind of subscription fee. Evangelization becomes membership recruitment and hospitality is degraded to making people comfortable.

We see the distortion when the measure of whether the parish is a "good community" is reduced to social life. The more times and the more members who gather for parish dinners become the measures of health. There's a false analogy behind that view. Maybe it's the false analogy that the church is a social club.

At the same time, we miss the point when we resist the parish's social life. Reversing the situation isn't any better. Negating people's desire for informal, "non-religious" time together is a denial of incarnational faith.

While the process of making analogies with these other groups is inevitable, and at times even useful, it also creates a problem. "People come to the conclusion that the Church is a 'society created by human enterprise and designed to serve particular human ends,' that it is created by the 'agreement of a number of individual persons who presumably define the terms of their association and its goals.' ...Church means, not corporation and not club, but a collection of people who have been called out together by a voice or a word or a summons which comes to them from outside."[70]

Pray for knowledge.

Trapped in the existing demand system

This was discussed in the first chapter. We can be unmindful of the web of expectations, pressures, and beliefs that inhibit our ability to do what's necessary for a healthier parish. We get driven along through the weeks and years by the routine demands of parish life. We assume there will be a time when we have the time to work on all the strategic and truly important developmental possibilities. It's a never-to-arrive point in the future.

Developmental work occurs when we make the developmental and strategic matters part of our demand system by doing things such as: creating a parish development team, using a skilled external consultant, having a yearly leadership retreat that is only about strategic and developmental concerns, and attending a program like Shaping the Parish™. Putting developmental activities on the parish schedule and weaving them into the fabric of parish life will create a new system of demands and expectations.

Pray for wisdom.

The parish priest engaging parishioners around their spiritual life

By ordination the priest carries the primary responsibility for the pastoral oversight of the parish church. The priest is there to shape the parish. Others may, and hopefully will, share in that ministry and collaborate with the priest. But finally the priest needs to accept this oversight role if the parish is to become healthier and more faithful.

In fact, a strong lay role in shaping the parish is unlikely if the priest fails to personally engage the oversight responsibility to "equip the saints for the work of ministry and the building up of his body." Roy Oswald of Alban Institute put it this way: "We have noted time and again the phenomenon in which the top leadership in an organization does not assume its rightful authority, with the result that others in the system are not able to assume their authority."

There are a variety of opportunities for the priest to engage the task.

Taking initiative with people

This means doing something many clergy avoid—opening up a conversation about the member's spiritual practices.

I believe that most people "want clergy to be interested in their spiritual life. The expectation may be strongest among those of Experimenting, Progressing and Apostolic Faith. They aren't

133

seeking an interrogation ('Do you pray?') but a sense of curiosity and an openness to listen. 'Tell me about your spiritual life,' 'I'd love to hear something about who the people were and are in your life who have helped you in your spiritual life.' "[71]

The Resources section of *Fill All Things* contains the "Three Interview Process." This has been used by participants in the Church Development Institute (CDI) to explore spiritual life with others in the parish. It's been used by hundreds of laity and clergy to provide a sense of safety for what is usually a very important conversation for both parties. Some clergy may find it helpful to have a routine that makes use of such a method with all new members. It could be part of early visiting as well as check-ins. It could be used in more structured settings such as Foundations Courses or parish orientation sessions and then followed up one-on-one.

What the priest wants to accomplish here is creating an unspoken psychological contract with new members that helps them know they can approach the priest about spiritual practice and allows the priest to more easily take initiative as circumstances allow or demand. It requires persistence and patience.[72]

Spontaneous opportunities

There are moments when it's right to ask a question, offer a brief thought, or invite a person to sit and talk. You might see the moment in curiosity or a new openness, an emotional outburst, or a change in behavior.

Offering group and individual guidance

I've heard some priests try to beg off from making such offerings because they don't have formal training in spiritual direction. While those with certificates and formal training are very helpful in this ministry, it remains true that providing spiritual guidance is part of the routine stuff of parish ministry. If you feel a need for special training, get it. If you feel out of your depth, pray and seek help. If you feel as though you are being arrogant, submit to spiritual guidance yourself.

For an outline of what could be provided see "Offering Spiritual Guidance in the Parish" in *Fill All Things*.

Confession[73]

Confession isn't the same thing as spiritual guidance but it is related. In parishes where the sacramental confession is routinely offered clergy are often surprised that if they do offer it, and educate about it, some will make use of the rite.

Minimally, it makes sense to occasionally note in the bulletin that it is available on request. Setting aside a few hours in Lent or Holy Week when the priest will be available at a specific location is also useful.

Guiding the parish as a whole

Pastoral oversight includes three dimensions of parish life: leadership, community, and spirituality.[74] Oversight is expressed as we seek to weave these three threads into the routine business of parish life. Oversight is about knitting things together in harmony and beauty.

Our oversight has the purpose of advancing the "holy order" of Christ. We are to enable a parish life in which people may rest in God, offer their lives to God, give themselves to the mission they share in the Body of Christ, and be transformed more and more into his likeness.

Each parish activity, all parish groups, every decision made, offers an opportunity for leadership and deeper community and spirituality. Of course, relentlessness about this will have the effect of damaging the parish's harmony. That can create a driven and sometimes hostile tone. We do need prudence, good sense, gentleness, and practical judgment, along with persistence. We need leadership grounded in truth and directed toward what is good for the parish and the person.

Some will want to aggressively recruit new members. Pastoral oversight will point to the organic evangelization of the Body of Christ and guide people into humility and patience. Some will want to fill Sunday morning with business meetings and education. Pastoral oversight will seek to create a climate of holiness and community. Some will want to ask 100% commitment and participation (the cause will vary from pledging to the potluck dinner). Pastoral oversight will suggest invitation and the wisdom to know there is never 100%.

Place the parish in a context of support, competency building, and accountability

You want to create a new "demand system" that draws the energies of the parish around the primary task, spiritual practices and other strategic matters. There are a few examples of turn-arounds without such support, but in such cases there is all too often a high cost in clergy over-functioning or conflict.

Consultants

Good consultants can provide a source for new energy and focus. It will be most effective if the consultation stretches over a period of at least 18 months or is a long weekend each year for three or four years. The form of consultation is, of course, critical.

Beware of consultants who have "the Answer" and are eager to provide you with a written report or program as the primary outcome. Effective consultants build the parish's internal capacity by leveraging their strengths in the service of your own development. For this kind of work, it is generally not helpful for an expert to provide the parish with a "solution" outside of itself.

Shaping the Parish^{TM}

I think what Michelle Heyne and I are doing in Shaping the Parish™ provides such a system. For a 16-month period, participants enter into a context that includes regular workshop time, six well-thought-out and planned parish initiatives, a course of readings, and support and guidance from peers and the training staff. The goal is to revitalize parishes.

We are confident that parishes sending a team that includes their priest are very likely to see early results after 16 months in the program. If they stay with what they have started, they will get healthier and might even generate the kind of energy that facilitates membership grow.

If they continue to use the program for several cycles we think most will find themselves in a significantly better place. See www.shapingtheparish.com.

There are other training programs in dioceses requiring a substantial investment of time and effort by parish leaders. The Church Development Institute is the program with the most experience, involving the largest number of people. Its focus is primarily on developing competent congregational development practitioners.

The diocese

The role of the diocese can be critical but is rarely enough in itself. The exceptions have often been in situations where the diocese had the authority to insist on participation in developmental processes. There are other cases where the bishop's office took a stance of persistent encouragement to help parishes enter into the needed context.

In the 60s and 70s, the Lutherans in Philadelphia created the Center City Lutheran Parish (CCLP).[75] Twenty-two churches participated. They all experienced increased health and growth. This was happening at the same time the Episcopal diocese in the city continued to close parish after parish.

Among the factors related to their success were: recruiting some of the best younger clergy right out of seminary[76]; leaving clergy in place for the long term, adequate funding for each parish over a significant period of time; a required weekly gathering of pastors for support and accountability, and the development of lay leaders.

In the 1980s I was the Congregational Development Officer in Connecticut. That position included oversight of all the aided congregations (all smaller parishes). We required all the aided parishes to meet together, engage in self and mutual assessment, have a three-party development agreement (vestry, priest, bishop's office), use a consultant, and for all new vicars to participate in what was an early form of CDI.

In a five-year period those parishes increased their average pledge by 68% and attendance by 15%. In congregations with leaders participating in the training program, the figures were 80% average pledge increase and 24% in attendance. All parishes reported increased satisfaction with the central elements of parish life, e.g., worship, formation, service, evangelization, etc. We did this while also decreasing the percentage of the diocesan budget used for financial aid to those parishes. It was also a time when the state's population was declining.

More recently the Diocese of Washington has followed a strategy of providing consulting and training resources along with interventions from the diocesan office to monitor development, facilitate decision making when hard choices were necessary, and provide empathetic support for parish leaders. When parish leaders give themselves to the process we see hope and less fear, new energy, health, and organic membership growth.

Perhaps we are waking up once again to the desire to make sense of the spiritual mysteries that sustained humanity for so many centuries.

Jonathan Aitken[77] in the *Daily Mail*, Christmas Eve 2009

Eight
Conclusion

A deep longing

I was surprised at the strong positive reaction to my presentation on spiritual practices at the Colorado CDI. It was the first time I had publicly shared what was to become the "map" for the *In Your Holy Spirit* books. It's not that I was expecting a negative reaction but I wasn't prepared for the strength of the confirmation that day. The conversation was lively and people came up to me later wanting to talk.

What I experienced that day was an excited longing. Since then I've seen the same response in parish vestries and retreats. One priest shared with me how important the work on spiritual practices had been for her and the parish. "It strikes a cord that seems familiar to people. Experiences they know about but have lost touch with." She went on to describe how the parish and individuals within the parish had reclaimed these practices of our tradition.

The practices of our tradition provide the grounding and integration many seek. For some it's like reconnecting with a lost friend; for others it's an expression of needs and emotions felt but not fully understood. Engaging the ancient practices in this new time continues to be a way to enter into the life of God, to have our hearts enlarged, to feel more connected and less alone, to believe in things seen and unseen, and to be open to the glory and mystery of life.

Waking up—it works

Ada Calhoun wrote about being "a closet Christian" in a December 2009 article on Salon. While Calhoun lives in Manhattan her views seem familiar to those of us living in Seattle. The full title of her article is "I am a closet Christian: At least, I was until now. Because in my circle, nothing is more embarrassing than being religious." For those of us living in the Northwest, it's a familiar attitude. I've heard the same view expressed by many people.

141

I came across a statement in the newspaper[78] saying that "studies have found that the rise in Evangelical Christianity is driving more moderate Christians to abandon religion altogether." I wonder about the relationship. Do the excesses of parts of evangelical Christianity produce such a reaction? Do more moderate people find themselves embarrassed to be seen as in the same camp? Calhoun wrote, "…[W]ho wants to be lumped in with all the other Christians, especially the ones you see on TV protesting gay marriage, giving money to charlatans, and letting priests molest children?"

Maybe there's a choice about direction there. We can either help people claim and become proficient in the spiritual life of our tradition, or some will move toward an expression that offers a clearer self-definition and others away from religious involvement entirely.

Jonathan Atkins wrote, "since coming out of prison almost ten years ago, I have been searching for and finding stronger spiritual foundations." He connects his own path with the signs he sees around him of a renewed openness to spiritual life, including religious life.

On Salon, Ada Calhoun noted her engagement with Judaism, Zen and Hinduism, Pure Land Buddhism and Gnosticism before she found herself an Episcopalian. Her way in was this: "The priest with whom my husband and I did premarital counseling had firsthand experience of closing bars, but he also was smart and eloquent and fulfilled. He showed me the best side of Christianity. Not how it's right or just, but how—and this may sound stupid, but it's what I think about religion in general—it *works*." She especially noted the comfort and rootedness she gained by being part of "an eternal community."

"It works." I think that's a reasonable understanding of what Karen Armstrong is saying when she writes of the confusion we have experienced about faith since turning it into a matter of belief instead of practice.[79] "If you don't 'do' religion—you don't 'get' it!"

The invitation of this book is for parish churches to become more traditional and more innovative, to give themselves to the ancient ways so they might better serve a new generation. To hold fast to the wisdom that what's happening in life is that the old is being made new, heaven is brought to earth, the human is made divine, and the glory of God is in human beings fully alive.

The doctrines are all enfleshed in practice—Incarnation is about love and human dignity, Trinity and Church are about community, the forgiveness of sins and resurrection of the dead is about hope in things unseen, and the Ascension is about the empowerment of a wounded humanity.

Paradox

As Bishop N.T. Wright puts it, "Christian virtue isn't about *you*—your happiness, your fulfillment, your self-realization. It's about God and God's kingdom, and your discovery of a genuine human existence by the paradoxical route—the route God himself took in Jesus Christ!—of giving yourself away, of generous love which constantly refuses to take center stage."[80]

Give yourself to generous love and find your happiness, fulfillment and self-realization along the way. Bishop Wright holds that we gain the "genuinely good human life" in a life "of character formed by God's promised future"…"lived within the ongoing story of God's people."[81] We find our life by losing our life. We discover our destiny by orienting ourselves to God's future. We become an individual by being part of a people.

Charles Williams was pointing in the same direction. "See, understand, enjoy, said the Gnostic, repent, believe, love, said the Church, and if you see anything by the way, say so." Williams was affirming what comes first and is the ground for all seeing, understanding and enjoyment.

Perfection

Thomas Merton wrote, "The perfect Christian is therefore not one who is necessarily impeccable and beyond all moral weakness; but he is one who, because his eyes are enlightened to know the full dimensions of the mercy of Christ, is no longer troubled by the sorrows and frailties of this present life. His confidence in God is perfect, because he '*knows*,' so to speak, by experience that God cannot fail him. …For such…lovers of God… All things manifest

143

the loving mercy of God. All things enable them to grow in love. All events serve to unite them to God."[82]

I think this was Julian's point:

> *All shall be well*
> *and all shall be well*
> *and all manner of thing shall be well*

It is exhibited in the image of Christ as shepherd. I stray, he seeks me and brings me home upon his shoulders. I face death, he is beside me to comfort. "Through all the length of days thy goodness faileth never."[83]

The parish church is a setting in which women and men might come to that place of confidence.

The Church

Jesus has given us the church, and in and through the church, sacraments, liturgy, scriptures, community, and ordained clergy. We are given all that so we may be in Christ and Christ in us.

This calls parish leaders to be clear in themselves and with others that the essential activities are not the budgets, programs, and goals of the institution. All too often people's energies are diverted into helping run the parish.

However necessary such efforts are, they do not make saints. Those who offer themselves for such work deserve special attention in the nurturing of their inner life. All the encounters, decisions, and conversation of their parish work are opportunities for growth. But the fulfillment of that possibility requires a sound grounding in spiritual practices, especially the daily practice of the Office and the capacity to be reflective.

Saints are made by God. Our call is to actively engage the pathways of grace that God has offered. Our growing union with

Christ is by way of our connection to him, in baptism, in and through the church. For most of us, that is in and through the parish church. It is in the sacrifice and compassion of a parish community that we grow. It is in the moments of mutual courage and perseverance, in the times of grace and beauty, that we grow. It is in loving and being loved that we grow.

We will enter into such opportunities as we are able. We will be as able as our growth up to that point permits. We don't get to jump beyond the history of our life. We are ready for what we are ready.

What we can do is put ourselves in the living waters of grace. Spiritual practices, living by Rule not rules, may help us cooperate in the process of sanctification.

Spiritual practices

My belief is that focusing on spiritual practice is the most efficient and effective way to form people in the Christian life, initially incorporate new members, and build a healthy parish culture.

There is of course more involved in parish health than just spiritual life. There needs to be alignment between income and expenses and of our hopes and visions with energy, facilities, and funds. There needs to be good leadership and emotional maturity. But it is spiritual life that is at the heart of why the parish church exists.

Imagination

Diana Butler Bass has made a significant contribution in providing images of healthy congregations. What struck me in her work was that these are churches not unlike most churches. They could be us.

What they have become and done is something we can be and do. Bass notes that it was her encounter with a particular church that "opened my imagination to the possibilities of what Christianity could be—a vibrant community of faith, traditional and innovative at the same time, based in Christian practice, and seeking a deeper way of wisdom."[84]

Many parish leaders need images of what a healthy, vital parish looks like. What does a five star parish look like? It's important to have several such images. If there's only one, we tend to copy. Books like Bass's help fill that need. Sending teams to visit such parishes can also help.

Brian McLaren's "Episcopal Moment" talk is another route into imagination. He has been telling Episcopalians we have some unique gifts and we need to build upon them. Some of his observations about us are an openness to mysticism, space for people to differ, and liturgy (beauty and participation). He affirmed, "In worship you actually do stuff."

The work done in strategic planning and strategy management over the years has consistently talked about the need to work off your strengths. It is also what those who work with Appreciative Inquiry claim. Start with the gifts you've been given. Begin with what you already know how to do well—expand and build upon it. That's the primary path to renewal.

That doesn't mean we can ignore the parish's weaknesses. A lack of proficiency in spiritual practices will result in a superficial life. Not facing into challenges that threaten the parish's integrity, identity or cohesion will eat away at the fabric of parish life. At the same time, compulsively trying to correct all imperfections is a kind of communal mental illness.

Faithful imagination begins with the gifts and graces already present and opens itself to new and more effective ways to live an ancient way.

Competence and long-term comfort rather than short-term comfort

The rector had become increasingly aware that there was a problem with too much care-taking of parishioners. He decided to change his practice during the Eucharist of giving instructions and specifically of asking people to sit for the reading. Accordingly, at the mid-week Eucharist he changed behavior and simply moved to sit down as the lector came forward to read.

Everyone in the congregation sat without instruction. Except John, who remained standing in the first pew. There he was—just standing. The rector, in his impulse to be kind, then stood halfway up and said, "We'll all sit for the reading." John then sat down.

It's an awkward dynamic. If you're going to allow people to become more responsible, empowered and participative, you must also allow them to suffer occasional moments of embarrassment.

If we are to allow people to grow we must *allow them* to be uncomfortable. That's not the same thing as *making them uncomfortable.*

Leadership

For the parish to become grounded in spiritual practices there's a need for the kind of leadership that knows how to navigate toward the destination. This is a lot about having political smarts— or what the behavioral scientists call emotional and social intelligence, and what the tradition refers to as gifts and virtues.

Shaping a parish for health and faithfulness involves practical judgment, justice, perseverance, self-awareness and control; it entails wisdom and spiritual maturity.

Parish leaders can begin by taking on the assumption that we are all unfinished. As individuals and as a parish, there is more to be and further to travel. That assumption is crucial. It opens up a new world.

This act of humility calls us into opportunities for growth as people and leaders. That will lead some to spiritual direction or therapy, others to a course of reading, some will work with parish consultants, and others will attend experiential training labs, Shaping the Parish™ or the Church Development Institute.

The development of a parish is a process of entering more deeply into the life of Christ and the nature and mission of the Church. A parish is being renewed as it enters into and reflects the mind, heart and work of Christ. A parish is being renewed as it enters into and reflects the unity, holiness, catholicity and apostolicity of the Church. A parish is being renewed as it pursues the mission of holy unity. Parish development is our striving, as a community of Christian people, toward God. It is not primarily something we do, or create, or make happen. It is the way in which a parish, a local manifestation of the Holy Catholic Church, shares in the Divine Life. It is living the Christian life, not simply as individuals, but as a people. The movement of a parish into a comprehensive and deep expression of the Christian Life is the result of years of striving, submitting and molding. It is the responsibility of clergy and lay leaders to monitor the life and ministry of, the parish and to take initiative in increasing the faithfulness and effectiveness of that life and ministry.

From *Power from on High*,
Robert A. Gallagher,
Ascension Press, 1983.

Nine

Resources

Orientation to Spiritual Practices

This is an example, in outline form, of such an orientation. It's an Anglican Spirituality program of three sessions. It's available at www.CongregationalDevelopment.com, "Parish Resources."

Prior to the class there is a Eucharist. Each session ends with Compline.

****

Advance Readings for First Session:

Episcopal Spirituality; The Christian Life Model: An Exploration; The Renewal—Apostolate Cycle; Tender Mercies; The Rule of St. Benedict: Roots of Anglican Spirituality.

First Session

- The balance, rhythm and dynamics of Anglican Spirituality
- Using the Daily Office—resources, methods

Advance Assignment for Second Session:

1. Experiment with some form of the daily office over next week.

2. Readings: The Threefold Rule of Prayer; The Eucharist: What Makes the Eucharist Effective in our Lives?; Eucharistic Spirituality, Practices and Traditions: #2, #4, #7; Several short pieces concerning Silence.

Second Session *(Most of the session will take place in the church)*

- Debrief—how did your use of the Daily Office go?

- In the church—walk through elements of the Eucharist, ways to more fully engage the Eucharist, such as silence, use of body, engaging the readings and sermon.

- If time permits: Worship styles in the Episcopal Church – what feeds you?

Advance Assignment for Third Session:

1. Experiment with participation in the Eucharist. Try something new at the next Eucharist that may enrich your worship.
2. Readings: The Threefold Rule of Prayer; Personal Devotions; Benedictine Teaching on Prayer; *Lectio Divina.*

Third Session

- Debrief what you did in the Eucharist.

- Experiment with various types of Personal Devotions

- Receive a worksheet for shaping your spiritual discipline (Rule of Life). See additional readings.

From *Anglican Spirituality Course* Copyright Robert A Gallagher & Michelle Heyne 2008. Available at www.CongregationalDevelopment.com

Assessing Your Spiritual Practices

SUNDAY EUCHARIST

1. Attendance (circle one)

About 1/4 of the time	Half the time	¾ of the time	Just about every Sunday

2. My ability to participate (Circle the number that is closest to your experience)

I am frequently confused and uncertain about how to participate				I can "flow" with it. I mostly don't need a Prayer Book or leaflet.
1	2	3	4	5

PARTICIPATING IN THE DAILY PRAYERS OF THE CHURCH

3. Doing the Office in some form on my own or with others

Never	Only when offered at a meeting or retreat	Sporadically or at during some season(s) of the church year	Most days

4. Knowing how to do the Daily Office

I have no idea.				I understand how to use it in the Prayer Book and ways to innovate the use
1	2	3	4	5

DISCIPLINED WAYS OF REFLECTING ["LISTEN TO YOUR LIFE"]

Grounding/centering yourself so you can reflect. The spiritual practice of "pondering" and seeking God's presence in the people, circumstances and things of life. Practices that connect daily life to God.

5. Ways that work for me

I don't have ways that work for me			I have ways that are effective for me
1	2	3	4	5

PARTICIPATING IN THE PARISH COMMUNITY

6. The community I seek is one in which people are free to be themselves; to speak and listen fully and authentically. In which differences are accepted (we can fight with those we love). In which we can make decisions and solve the problems we face.

I don't want church to be that way			It is what I seek; and more
1	2	3	4	5

7. Connection with people

I don't know anyone well			I know a number of people and have a few friends in the parish
1	2	3	4	5

8. Participation in parish social life

Not at all				I participate regularly and frequently
1	2	3	4	5

SERVICE

9. In Daily Life

I don't have a clear understanding of how I serve in my daily life				I am very clear about serving in daily life
1	2	3	4	5

THE PROCESS OF SPIRITUAL GROWTH

10. Foundations

I have a poor foundation in the spiritual practices of the church				I have a strong foundation in the spiritual practices of the church
1	2	3	4	5

11. Experiment

I don't know how or feel confident enough to experiment with spiritual practices			I have a sense of how to innovate & experiment with spiritual practices.	
1	2	3	4	5

Resources
Assessing the Parish's Spiritual Practices

Your name: _____

A. Your Attendance at the Sunday Eucharist (circle one)

About 1/4 of the time	Half the time	¾ of the time	Just about every Sunday

B. Your Spiritual Discipline—I have a spiritual disciple grounded in the church's tradition

No				Very much so
1	2	3	4	5

OVERALL

1. The degree of awareness of spiritual practices **and proficiency** among regular attendees (circle one)

No idea	15% of the adult average Sunday attendees are aware of the core spiritual practices and few are proficient	40% of the adult average Sunday attendees are aware of the core spiritual practices and 5% are proficient	80% of the adult average Sunday attendees are aware of the core spiritual practices and 30% are proficient

SUNDAY EUCHARIST[1]

2. Members' ability to participate

Most are frequently confused and uncertain about how to participate.			A critical mass of people "flow" with it. Mostly don't need a Prayer Book or leaflet.	
1	2	3	4	5

3. Congregation or audience

We are like an audience. We wait for instructions and prompting before participating.			We are a congregation— competent in the liturgy. There are no instructions during the Eucharist.	
1	2	3	4	5

4. Competence of liturgical assistants—We effectively equip those with a special role in the celebration, e.g., cantor, lector, ministers of the altar, acolyte.

We do a poor job			Done well	
1	2	3	4	5

---

[1] There is a longer Eucharistic Assessment available in Robert Gallagher's *Eucharistic Spirituality: From Audience to Congregation*, Ascension Press, 2011

5. Liturgical presence of the presiding priest—A sacramental presence. The person and the role are held together. The priest's personality doesn't overwhelm the role; the role doesn't make the personality disappear. Graceful, attentive.

Awful				Done well
1	2	3	4	5

6. The liturgy is usually well done. It has the structure, climate and rhythm of Apostolic faith. It requires some competence. It has the potential to catch people up in something beyond themselves; to feed wonder and awe. The congregation knows how to participate without prompting.

Not at all				Very much so
1	2	3	4	5

7. The **preaching** usually has a good pace, style, sense of ease, and length. It connects the tradition with life. There is an authenticity about the preacher and what is said.

Not at all				Very much so
1	2	3	4	5

8. The **Liturgical Space** is graceful, not cluttered; is beautiful; fits the congregation's size and style of worship. Those serving at the altar can move about without awkwardness.

Not at all				Very much so
1	2	3	4	5

9. The Holy Eucharist is celebrated on **enough occasions**, at times each week as to allow people with a variety of schedules to find one that might serve as their weekly spiritual practice.

Not at all				Very much so
1	2	3	4	5

PARTICIPATING IN THE DAILY PRAYERS OF THE CHURCH

10. The parish offers a **public form of the Daily Office**

Never	Sporadically or at during some season(s) of the church year	A few days each week	Most days of the week

11. Those **participating in officiating** at the parish's public offering of the Daily Office are:

There is no public offering of the Office			Both clergy and lay members officiate on a regular basis	
1	2	3	4	5

12. The **parish equips and supports** parishioners in saying the Daily Prayer of the Church on their own in the course of daily life by offering training and guidance.

Not at all			Regular and frequent training and guidance are provided	
1	2	3	4	5

13. 15 – 20% of those regularly attending a weekly Eucharist **say the Office in some form.**

Few or none in the parish say the Office			At least that many	
1	2	3	4	5

DISCIPLINED WAYS OF REFLECTING

14. The **parish provides members assistance** in identifying and maintaining ways of being reflective.

Not at all			Regularly	
1	2	3	4	5

15. The parish **engages in reflective processes,** ways of listening to and learning from its own life as a community.

Not at all			Regularly	
1	2	3	4	5

16. The parish's reflective processes have helped it **become more flexible and adaptive.**

Not at all			Very much so	
1	2	3	4	5

PARTICIPATING IN THE PARISH COMMUNITY

17. This is a parish community in which people are free to be themselves; to speak and listen fully and authentically. In which differences are accepted (we can fight with those we love). In which we can make decisions and solve the problems we face.

Not at all				Very much so
1	2	3	4	5

18. Connection with people.

Most don't know anyone well				Regular attendees usually know a number of people and have a few friends in the parish
1	2	3	4	5

19. Participation in parish social life is easy for members to engage. The climate is one of acceptance whether you participate or not.

Not at all				Very much so
1	2	3	4	5

SERVICE

20. Service in Daily Life (within our friendships, families, work, and civic life):

Few have a clear understanding of how they serve in daily life			Most regular attendees are very clear about service in daily life	
1	2	3	4	5

21. As a parish community we have a form of serving beyond the parish's needs that is **sustainable and in proportion** to what we can manage.

We are overwhelmed by it			It's easily managed	
1	2	3	4	5

22. Our parish's corporate service ministry **fits our gifts** as a parish.

Not a fit			Fits us	
1	2	3	4	5

The Process of Change

The parish can also model an approach to change or experimentation and learning from experience. It can teach methods that allow people to face change

23. An adult foundations course is offered regularly and frequently in the parish.

Never			Regular & frequent	
1	2	3	4	5

24. The parish has a climate and an approach to the spiritual life that encourages **experimentation *and* the engagement** of the tradition.

Not the case			Very much so	
1	2	3	4	5

The Renewal—Apostolate Cycle

The Renewal - Apostolate Cycle is a way of describing a central dynamic of Christian life. The Cycle focuses our attention on the Christian's movement between being renewed in baptismal identity and purpose and living as instruments of God's love and grace in daily life. The Cycle is interested in both the individual's movement and in the ways in which the parish church supports and facilitates that movement. This is the primary task of any parish church.

RENEWAL

Renewal in baptismal identity and purpose in worship, study, the parish's social life, and being equipped for Christian action

APOSTOLATE

Participation in the work of Christ in service, evangelization and stewardship
In areas of:
 Workplace, Civic Life,
 Family & Friends,

A Cycle

The cycle is between a conscious and intentional attention to God, prayer life, our relationships, Christian formation **and** a subconscious reliance upon God as members of the Body of Christ, in the workplace, family, friendship, civic life and congregational life.

In that Cycle:

We need:	Which is helped by:	Which the parish helps by:
To accept our dependence on God	Openness to spiritual guidance	An emphasis in its life on worship; nothing comes before the Eucharist and Daily Office. Also, more attention to formation and spiritual growth than other programs or ministries.
To accept responsibility for ordering our spiritual life	Establishing a rule of life	Offering programs and guidance in creating, experimenting with, and revising a spiritual discipline.
To accept our interdependence with others in the Church	Life in Christian community, a parish church	Being a healthy and faithful parish church and by helping people relate to the parish community in ways appropriate to their personality and the parish's capacities. Having opportunities for social life and the development of friendships.

From *Fill All Things: The Spiritual Dynamics of the Parish Church,* Robert A Gallagher, Ascension Press, 2008

Shape of the Parish Model

The model can be used: to assess the health of a parish, and in developing a strategy that deepens the parish's spiritual life, while staying open to the various places people are in their faith journey.

From *Fill All Things: The Spiritual Dynamics of the Parish Church* Robert A. Gallagher Copyright 2008. "Shape of the Parish" Diagram, Robert A. Gallagher/Mary Anne Mann, 1983; Revised RAG 1999, 2003.

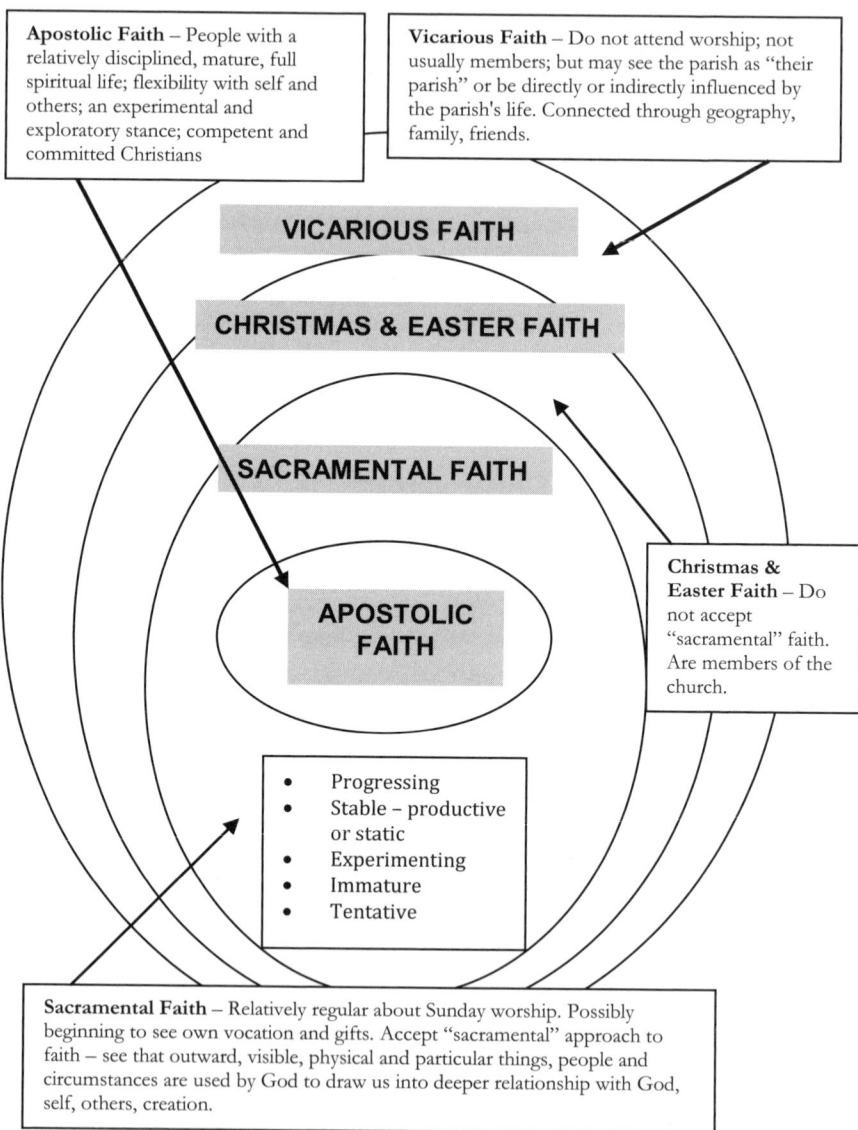

Apostolic Faith – People with a relatively disciplined, mature, full spiritual life; flexibility with self and others; an experimental and exploratory stance; competent and committed Christians

Vicarious Faith – Do not attend worship; not usually members; but may see the parish as "their parish" or be directly or indirectly influenced by the parish's life. Connected through geography, family, friends.

VICARIOUS FAITH

CHRISTMAS & EASTER FAITH

SACRAMENTAL FAITH

APOSTOLIC FAITH

Christmas & Easter Faith – Do not accept "sacramental" faith. Are members of the church.

- Progressing
- Stable – productive or static
- Experimenting
- Immature
- Tentative

Sacramental Faith – Relatively regular about Sunday worship. Possibly beginning to see own vocation and gifts. Accept "sacramental" approach to faith – see that outward, visible, physical and particular things, people and circumstances are used by God to draw us into deeper relationship with God, self, others, creation.

More on Shaping the Parish

The following is excerpted from *Fill All Things* as noted.

Critical mass models draw the attention of leaders away from obsessing about "fixing" the problems and dysfunction at the edges and toward building the center. We can all too easily find our attention drawn toward the "difficult people" or those who constantly demand personal attention. A critical mass model suggests that we give much more of our time and energy to developing the center by equipping those already of Apostolic Faith and those ready to move in that direction.[85]

When a parish has a healthy and productive Shape you see a definite movement. People are drawn into a deeper relationship with God and the church. There is a sense of spiritual movement in the parish.[86]

Leaders are establishing two dynamics at the center in shaping the parish. They are the deep underlying assumptions that provide the base for a healthy parish culture. The parish church is about forming people for "real life;" for maturity in Christ. It is developing in women and men a taste for life in what John Macquarrie saw as "a commonwealth of free, responsible beings united in love." Secondly, the parish is about engaging "an energy not its own." Formation isn't about creating perfect, sinless people. It is about connecting us to the power of the Holy Spirit.[87]

General Comments on Nurturing Growth

1. The core pastoral strategy is to **accept** people where they are *and* to **invite** them to move beyond where they are.

2. Individual growth often comes in leaps (e.g., a person may move quickly from Experimenting to Progressing to Apostolic Faith).

3. Foundations are important. At times there is a desire to grow, or there may be deep feeling about God and/or the church. Such feelings can be the pastor's opening to invite the person into a setting where the needed base is offered. That foundation in spiritual life or knowledge may serve the person ten years later when they are prepared to move more deeply into the relationship with God and the church.

4. Address the gaps that people live in. The gap may be between the person's intentions and the impact of their behavior on others. There may be gaps of understanding more common to some forms of faith than others. The "Believing—Belonging" gaps may be especially strong in people of Vicarious and C&E Faith. The gap between faith and daily life may be common in the phases of Vicarious, C&E and early Sacramental faith.

5. New members need special attention. They may be people transferring from other parishes who already live an Apostolic or Stable Sacramental Faith. They might be C&E or people who for some reason have decided to begin attending. Or they could be people with almost no religious background, without any connection to the parish, who have just decided to "try it." Often these people may come with a good bit of emotional intelligence, a strong longing, and good intentions but lack foundational practices. There is the potential that they might move quickly into a progressing expression of Sacramental faith.[88]

Many of the assumptions of this approach are seen in other places:

> You can see the same orientation when Bishop Kilmer Myers wrote in *Light the Dark Streets*, "One possible definition for a parish is that it is God's way of meeting the problems of the unloved. This meeting between God and the unloved, the unwanted, takes place in the preaching of the Word, in the Sacraments, in the social life of the parish made possible by the climate of acceptance which is engendered by those who have been baptized and confirmed in the Catholic faith. One of the main tasks of the parish priest is to train the militant core of his parishioners in such a way that they understand as fully as possible the true nature of a Christian parish."

> In *Pastoral Theology: A Reorientation* Martin Thornton presented his understanding of the parish church as the Body of Christ, "the complete Body in microcosm," (p. 19) and his Remnant Concept, "in which power from the center pervades the whole." (p. 21) The holiness and love of a Remnant at the center of parish life is for Thornton what makes a parish a true parish. In describing how the Remnant Concept works he writes: "This palpitating heart pumps the blood of life to all the body as leaven leavens the lump or salt savours the whole." (p. 23)

Notes

[1] Mental models—"The image of the world around us, which we carry in our head, is just a model. Nobody in his head imagines all the world, government or country. He has only selected concepts, and relationships between them, and uses those to represent the real system." (Jay Wright Forrester) Everyone has mental models. It's part of how we make sense of and give order to our world. They simplify reality. Our understanding of ourselves, others, the work we do, and what information is important largely depends on how we have conceptualized our experience. We have created a kind of subconscious hypothesis about how things work. They are necessarily based on incomplete information coming from the limitations of a person or group's experience. It's selective perception. The parish can expand its mental models by: 1) increased awareness of the existing models and the assumptions around them; 2) using models of system dynamics such as a group development theory, a spiritual map, or something like the Shape of the Parish, or the Creeds of the church; and 3) attention to the way in which the parish learns from its experience. The way of learning involved is a shift from what has been called "single-loop learning" to "double-loop learning." That's a shift from a static view of things to one that takes into account the actual dynamics, the related results and changes, and explicit mental models in the form of theories or frameworks.

[2] Diana Butler Bass, *Christianity for the Rest of Us*, Harper One, 2006, page 284.

[3] In *Fill All Things: The Spiritual Dynamics of the Parish Church*, Robert A. Gallagher, Ascension Press, 2008, Chapter IV. Further references will simply cite "Fill All Things."

[4] Ibid, page 142.

[5] Ibid, page 156.

[6] "The primary task is the most important and essential process an organization uses in fulfilling its mission. For example, for years Loren Mead and others have been proposing that the primary task of a diocese is congregational development. I think that's correct. ... Being clear about the organization's primary task is essential if we are to focus resources in the service of mission. Some people in the business community talk about 'stacking resources toward success.' That has to do with placing your human, material and financial resources in service of the primary things you are trying to accomplish. Primary task clarity allows us to stack our resources.

What is the primary thing that a parish church does toward fulfilling the mission? What is it that a parish is especially suited for, organically created for? My view is that the parish church's primary task is the renewal of baptismal identity and purpose in those related to the parish. The baptismal and Eucharistic community is about Glory, giving glory to God in liturgy and in human lives that are "real lives," fully alive lives. The parish is a community and a place in which people share in the Glory of God. All of which is to say that the primary task of a parish is worship – it is adoration, reverence, devotion, and love. From *Fill All Things,* Pages 11 – 12.

[7] *Fill All Things,* page 57.

[8] Psalm 78, "For he remembered that they were but flesh, * a breath that goes forth and does not return."

[9] Aidan Kavanagh wrote, "Solemnity should skip rather than trundle, dance rather than lumber. Solemnity and simplicity are close to being the same thing, and each is native to a liturgy which is divine service." My hunch is that real boredom with the Liturgy coincides with a lack of solemnity and the increased use of dull, commonplace liturgical art.

[10] A booklet on Liturgical Presence is available at www.CongregationalDevelopment.com in the Parish Resources section. It offers ideas about both behaviors and a stance that assist in maintaining a liturgical presence. Includes items on physical bearing, movement, humility, and non-anxious presence.

[11] "Eucharistic Practices: Notes for Facilitators" is an educational design to introduce people to spiritual practices commonly used by members of the congregation. It is available at www.congregationaldevelopment.com in the Parish Resources section.

[12] Booklets on "Liturgical Presence" and "Practices During the Holy Eucharist" are available at www.congregationaldevelopment.com in the Parish Resources section. The same material is available in *Eucharistic Spirituality: From Audience to Congregation*, Robert A Gallagher, Ascension Press, 2011.

[13] "Howard Galley, in his book *The Ceremonies of the Eucharist*, gives us an image of the people coming forward.

The approach of the people is properly understood as a kind of procession: those in the front of the church going forward first, followed by those in the seats behind them in a steady stream. It is far better that there should be many people waiting in the aisle than to create the impression that the

> *communicants are approaching in "groups" or "blocks" of individuals.*

This image emphasizes the congregation as representative of the Body of Christ, and also speaks to our eagerness to participate in the Sacrament—spilling out into the aisles on our own volition, active participants in the liturgy." Excerpted from "Communion at Trinity," by Michelle Heyne.

[14] From Robert A. Gallagher, *Eucharistic Spirituality: From Audience to Congregation*, Ascension Press, 2011 (earlier copyrights 2002, 2009). "It is important to note that the norm for receiving is to receive both bread and wine; and to receive from the common cup. Intinction is the practice of the bread being dipped into the wine and then consumed. The practice is primarily a 19th century development based on spiritual confusion and some false assumptions about hygiene. It is a permissible practice; especially when you have a cold or some other illness and you wish to avoid any danger of passing it to others. A possible preferable practice is to receive only the bread; leaving the rail before the cup is administered or giving a slight shake of the head as the minister of communion approaches.

The best practice for receiving by intinction (for reasons of both hygiene and spirituality) is to leave the bread in the palm of your hand; this signals the minister of communion about your intentions; the priest or chalice-bearer can then take the host from your fingers, dip it slightly into the wine and place it on your tongue. Among the issues to consider:

1. Our Mission - The sacrament is a means given to fulfill the mission of Christ and the Church, e.g., our restoration to unity with one another and God. In part this is about our relationship to each other. Sharing the common cup as an act of commitment to one another. There is also the history of the practice to consider. The claim of "hygiene" has often been a cover for other motives that fracture our unity. Class and race bias have played a significant role in the practice. This is an indication of the value of the sharing of the common cup.

2. Receiving. In our relationship with God we need to receive rather than to take control. We come to God in our need and hunger, in openness and humility. We need to receive.

3. Health. The Lutheran and Roman Catholic Churches have researched the issue and found no health problems associated with the common cup. The primary health concern that was identified was in an Anglican Church of Canada report, "Eucharistic Practice and the Risk of Infection." The report noted that there is much more of a health danger by allowing a

number of people to individually dip their bread into the common cup. "Medically we know that hands are much worse as transmitters of infection than lips."

4. Living in the Complexity of Life. Have you noticed the research about how children need exposure to germs, animal hair and dust in order to develop some resistance? Also, a report that Episcopal clergy have the second longest life expectancy of any professional group in the U.S. Sharing all of life with others may have physical as well as spiritual benefits.

[15] For more on the Daily Office see *Fill All Things,* pages 59 - 61 and 169 – 178. There's information on the rationale for the Office, the place of the Office in congregational development, and how to strengthen the place of the Office in parish life.

[16] Robert Benson, *In Constant Prayer,* published 2008 by Thomas Nelson, Inc.

[17] The value of the Office is its objectivity. It is a means by which we pray with the whole church, uniting our prayer with that of millions of other Christians living and dead. This is true whether one is alone or in a group, for the Office is essentially a corporate act. It is objective too in that it does not depend on our feelings, but gives our prayer life a regularity and a disciplined framework. Kenneth Leech, *True Prayer*

[18] "Our vocation is not simply to be, but to work together with God in the creation of our own life, our own identity, our own destiny—to work out our own identity in God, which the Bible calls 'working out salvation,' is a labor which requires sacrifice and anguish, risk and many tears." Thomas Merton

[19] "Prayer must involve the unifying of the personality, the integration of mind and heart into one center…. Without self discovery there can be no further progress. 'In order to find God whom we can only find in and through the depths of our own soul, we must first find ourselves.' Without self-knowledge our love remains superficial." Kenneth Leech, *Soul Friend)*

[20] St. Irenaeus, and St. Athanasius of Alexandria. Along the same lines Lancelot Andrewes wrote, "Whereby, as before He of ours, so now we of His are made partakers. He clothed with our flesh, and we invested with His Spirit. The great promise of the Old Testament accomplished, that He should partake our human nature; and the great and precious promise of the New, that we should be *'consortes divinae naturae', 'partake his divine nature,'* both are this day accomplished." The traditional prayer said by the deacon or priest when preparing the chalice is "By the mystery of this

water and wine may we come to share in the divinity of Christ who humbled himself to share in our humanity."

[21] Dietrich Bonhoeffer, *Letters and Papers from Prison*.

[22] Martin Thornton, *Christian Proficiency*.

[23] "we see through a glass, darkly" I Cor. 13:12.

[24] John Macquarrie, *Principles of Christian Theology*.

[25] David Brooks, "The Summoned Self," *The New York Times*, August 3, 2010.

[26] Larry Blumenfeld, "In Jazz, as in Life, Choices," *Wall Street Journal*, 11/5/09.

[27] John Neville Figgis, C.R. (1866 - 1919) was a monk in the Community of the Resurrection at Mirfield; a historian, political philosopher. The Community of the Resurrection was founded in 1892 by Charles Gore, Walter Howard Frere and others. It had a significant influence in the development of the Anglican Church in South Africa, through its school, in the ministry of Trevor Huddleston, CR, in his resistance to the destruction of Sophiatown, and in the influence of Huddleston and the Community of the Resurrection on Desmond Tutu.

[28] From the lives and times of archy and mehitabel, Don Marquis, Doubleday, 1916, 1927. The whole poem, "the lesson of the moth" is on the web at www.donmarquis.com/archy/. Archy is a cockroach, Mehitabel's a cat. The author reports that "Archy writes without punctuation because he is forced to use his head to butt the keys of the typewriter one at a time, and he is not able to reach the shift keys of the machine in order to make punctuation marks or capital letters. Mehitabel does not use the typewriting machine at all, so Archy is forced to be her reporter."

[29] *The New York Times*, August 27, 2009.

[30] See Stephen Covey, *The Seven Habits of Highly Effective People* and *First Things First*.

[31] Lab training has a goal of increasing the person's options for effective behavior in interpersonal, group, and organizational settings. The process involves disciplined reflection on the immediate here-and-now experiences within the learning community. Use is made of applied behavioral science theory to explore the patterns and dynamics present in a group or organization.

[32] LTI is part of the Church Development Institute system. See its web pages at www.CongregationalDevelopment.com.

Notes

33 *Shaping the Parish* focuses on making immediate, tangible improvements in the parish while building long-term health. For more information go to: www.ShapingtheParish.com.

34 As I recall, Cooperrider convinced the hotel to send key employees to a five star hotel to be in residence and talk with employees. The idea was to give them images they could work with to improve their own hotel. It can be an effective method for parishes. I've asked client parishes interested in improving liturgy or the formation of children to go to three places known for that area of parish life. They were to experience what the other parishes did and talk with leaders.

35 K.H. Ting was an Anglican Bishop in China and a leader of the China Christian Council.

36 *Fill All Things*, page 125.

37 In *Light the Dark Streets*, Kilmer Myers wrote, "One possible definition for a parish is that it is God's way of meeting the problems of the unloved. This meeting between God and the unloved, the unwanted, takes place in the preaching of the Word, in the Sacraments, in the social life of the parish made possible by the climate of acceptance which is engendered by those who have been baptized and confirmed in the Catholic faith. One of the main tasks of the parish priest is to train the militant core of his parishioners in such a way that they understand as fully as possible the true nature of a Christian parish."

38 *Pastoral Theology: A Reorientation* by Martin Thornton, SPCK, 1961, p. 19 and 21. Also issued by Cowley Publishing as *The Heart of the Parish: Theology of the Remnant*, 1989. In describing how the Remnant Concept works he writes: "This palpitating heart pumps the blood of life to all the body as leaven leavens the lump or salt savours the whole." (page 23)

39 See in *Fill All Things*, "Distortions of the Shape" pages 140 – 141 and "The Dynamic of the Shape" pages 142 – 146.

40 A sermon preached in the Chapel of the Good Shepherd at General Theological Seminary on January 30, 1988, for the Reception of the Promises of the Members, Companions and Associates of the Order of the Ascension.

41 For an exploration of friendship as part of the Christian life see *Fill All Things*, pages 27 – 31. "Parish churches are for many people a place of friendship. Some people are first attracted to a parish in the hope of meeting people and developing friendships. The connections begun in liturgy, classes and parish social gatherings are frequently extended into dinner together, time in a coffee shop or tavern, or brunch after the Sunday Eucharist. We might pick up on Aelred's thinking about how a Christian community can be a 'school of love.' For him the monastic

173

community was not only Benedict's "school for the Lord's service," it was also a 'school of love.' " Paul saw the local church in such terms, " And may the Lord make you increase and abound in love for one another and for all" (1 Thessalonians 3:12).

Occasionally in Christian life there are friendships of special intensity and depth. The church has sometimes acted in two broad ways when they are between people who could be romantic or sexual partners, but are not. One response has been an attempt to forbid and control it because it creates discomfort among some people. The other has been to see it as a category of relationship. The church has a long history of acknowledging special relationships by creating such categories. That's what religious orders such as the Benedictines and Franciscans represent. It's what solitaries and anchorites represent. Many bishops also continue to have uncertain feelings about these categories that in fact operate outside their usual controls.

In friendships that could be sexual or romantic, but aren't, the church has used categories such as: 1) spiritual marriage; a practice in which a man and a woman live intimately without having any sexual relationship; 2) spiritual friendship, where there is intimacy and a connecting of souls, where deep acceptance stands alongside a challenge to grow. Aelred of Rievaulx looked for four qualities--loyalty, right intention, discretion and patience; and 3) Charles Williams' idea of "companions," which was for him bound up with his idea of co-inherence: we exist in essential relationship with one another, as natural parts of one other. The idea of co-inherence includes *exchange*, in which we live in and from Christ and each other; *substitution*, in which we bear one another's burdens, cares, pain, and anxieties; and *romantic theology*, in which our worldly loves are seen as a reflection of heavenly love. Co-inherence includes our participation in Christ's death and resurrection, the workings of the city (and Holy City), the two natures of Christ (human and divine), the presence of Christ in the Eucharist, and all types of love.

[42] See the discussion on "Accepting the Human and the Symbol" in *Fill All Things,* pages 148 – 151.

Close friendships between clergy and parishioners have become increasingly problematic. Many clergy avoid any friendships within the parish. This of course undermines the healthy functioning of the parish community. Some avoid friendships because they require too much emotional intelligence to manage, others because the less mature in the parish may create a drama around their inclusion problems, and still others because the church's canons and guidelines make it possible for a third party to file a complaint against a priest in a close friendship when the lay person in the friendship is of the same sexual orientation. In spite of all this most clergy will have friendships within the parish, some of them close. In many of those cases the priest will have technically violated canons and guidelines. The day will come, of course, when this abusive pendulum swing will pass. The church's legacy of heresy trials, witch-hunts, and inquisitions is always present like a shadow and always done in the pursuit of some good. The need is to sort the good from that legacy. The church needs to join all other institutions in not allowing sexual abuse, harassment and exploitation. And we need to do that in a way that is just and doesn't interfere with the appropriate friendships of parish life.

[43] *The New York Times*, August 3, 2010. "Not on the Doctor's Check List, but Touch Matters."

[44] "Should We Be Growing?" Alice Mann, writing in *Alban Weekly*, May 10, 2010.

[45] P 496 *The Conservative Mind*, Russell Kirk.

[46] For more of an explanation of the virtues and gifts of the Holy Spirit see p. 163 in *Fill All Things*.

[47] Resources on theory and methods are in *Interventions: Methods and Processes for Building Healthier Parishes*, Michelle Heyne & Robert Gallagher, Ascension Press, 2011. Others are available at www.CongregationalDevelopment.com in the Parish Resources section and at www.ShapingTheParish.com in the Resources section.

[48] Based on "Trust Development in Organizations," Robert Gallagher, 1995. For more on the model see *Interventions: Methods and Processes for Building Healthier Parishes*, Michelle Heyne & Robert Gallagher, Ascension Press, 2011.

[49] *Community: The Structure of Belonging*, Peter Block, Berrett-Koehler Publ., San Francisco, 2008.

[50] Helene Oswald in MATC's—*Human Interaction Experiences: A Resource Book*, 1984.

[51] *Intervention Theory and Method: A Behavioral Science View*, Chris Argyris, Addison-Wesley, 1970.

[52] *The New York Times*, September 1, 2010 and "The power of teamwork" by Wallace Immen in *The Globe and Mail*, October 14, 2010. In Immen's article he offered take-away messages about teamwork based on the miner's experience. One was "We're in This Together." He wrote, "The miners realized from the start that rather than putting their own needs first, they had to work together, and depend on each other to survive; once contact

was made with rescuers, they became part of the overall effort to bring them out alive. In a show of solidarity, the miners vied with each other to be the final one to leave the cavern. Those with medical conditions were given extra consideration and rescued early, while the shift boss – the manager – was the last to leave."

[53] For more detail on testing processes see pages 109 – 110 in *Fill All Things*. "A testing process helps a community cope with situations in which a few persistent voices press a concern or idea that would have an effect on the community's life. What they are saying may represent a widely shared view or it may simply be their view. ... The use of a 'testing process' requires leaders to use sound judgment in deciding when the process is likely to produce valid and useful information as well as help the community manage its anxiety."

[54] Chapter 14, *Community: The Structure of Belonging*, Peter Block, Berrett-Koehler Publ., San Francisco, 2008.

[55] Mark Gibbs, "The Structures of the Church and the Different Kinds of Laity," Audenshaw Papers #26, 1974.

[56] The quotations are respectively from *Christianity and Social Order: What Christians Stand for in the Secular World*. There's a summary of Temple's views about the church's influence in society in *Fill All Things*, page 167.

[57] As a starting place see "The Church's Influence in Society" in *Fill All Things*, pages 167 – 168. William Temple wrote "The world...results from His love; creation is a kind of overflow of the divine love." And "The aim of a Christian social order is the fullest possible development of individual personality in the widest and deepest possible fellowship."

[58] Evelyn Underhill, *Concerning the Inner Life*.

[59] William Temple, *What Christians Stand for in the Secular World*.

[60] Thomas Oden, *Care of Souls in the Classic Tradition*.

[61] *The New York Times*, September 20, 2009.

[62] Carol Ann Duffy wrote a poem, "Last Post," to honor Patch and others, *You lean against a wall, your several million lives still possible and crammed with love, work, children, talent, English beer, good food. You see the poet tuck away his pocket-book and smile. If poetry could truly tell it backwards, then it would.*

[63] In his Rule, Benedict wrote, "have death at all times before one's eyes." Phil Ochs offered his own meditation on living in the face of death in his folksong, "When I'm Gone." David Steindl-Rast, OSB wrote, "It isn't primarily a practice of thinking of one's last hour, or of death as a physical phenomenon; it is a seeing of every moment of life against the horizon of death, and a challenge to incorporate that awareness of dying into every moment so as to become more fully alive."

[64] *Connected: The Surprising Power of Our Social Networks and How They Shape Our Lives*, Nicholas Christakis and James Fowler, Little, Brown and Company, 2009. page 30.

[65] *The Tipping Point: How Little Things Can Make a Big Difference* , Malcolm Gladwell, Little Brown, 2000.

[66] A foundations course is a substantial educational and training program that is repeated over the years and is used to incorporate people into the parish and the spirituality of the Episcopal Church. A foundations course is a resource for setting loose an energy in individuals and the parish that can stir new thinking and behavior and may help move some people into a more Apostolic expression of faith and practice. There needs to be enough substance to it that it has the potential of taking participants to a new place in their spiritual life. Some parishes have nine or ten sessions. Others have modules that extend over three years. It's a resource for:

- People exploring faith and spiritual life
- People joining the parish and/or the Episcopal Church
- Existing members who have not engaged these issues in recent years
- Adults preparing for baptism, confirmation, reception, or reaffirmation
- New comers who want to connect to the parish and meet other people

[67] Reframing or cognitive reframing is a method of changing the way we look at things and developing alternative ways of explaining and dealing with situations.

[68] *The New York Times*, September 5, 2010, "America's History of Fear," by Nicholas D. Kristof.

[69] See *Fill All Things*, pages 7, 23, 49 and 200.

[70] Richard Norris, *Understanding the Faith of the Church*, Seabury Press, NY, 1979.

[71] *Fill All Things* page 150.

[72] Proclaim the message; be persistent whether the time is favorable or unfavorable; convince, rebuke, and encourage, with the utmost patience in teaching 2 Timothy 4:2.

[73] "The Reconciliation of a Penitent" (BCP p.448).

[74] See *Fill All Things*, pages 82 – 85, 197 – 199.

[75] In 1981 I wrote a Forward Movement booklet, "Stay in the City," that proposed a strategy for the health and growth of inner city parishes. It included the following. In the 1960s and 70s in Philadelphia the Episcopalians continued a close city parishes strategy while the Lutherans

went in another direction. In the case of the Episcopalians, "Since 1940 we have seen the death of almost one congregation per year in the City of Philadelphia. Between 1900 and 1940 we averaged one closing or merger every other year. Sixty parishes in eighty years."

The Lutherans had a comparable situation. In a 1975 Synod report they painted this picture, "In one generation inner city Philadelphia churches had dwindled from 46 to 26. … It was obvious that unless something drastic were done, there would be little or no Lutheran witness within another generation." The Synod's response was this, "In the fall of 1964, inner city churches were invited to participate in the newly formed Center City Lutheran Parish (CCLP). Twenty-two joined. Each parish remained autonomous with their own council, control of finances, and normally their own pastor. Respect was shown for the ability of each pastor and council to know its own parish best needs best. CCLP provided assistance in responding to those needs, and a context of accountability and direction in regard to basic standards."

"Since 1964 (up till 1981), none of the parishes have closed. Black baptized membership went from about 500 to 3400. … Emergency food centers were established, major work with youth has been started, congregations are involved in the issues of their communities, the Director has been involved in city-wide issues, the giving of members has increased. A report in the mid 70s identified these factors as connected to the success of the effort: 1. Long-term, experienced pastors whose efforts were not interrupted by long vacancies. 2. Adequate funding – A significant period of time was guaranteed each parish. None of this 'turn things around in three years' stuff. 3. A weekly gathering of pastors - a support/accountability system 4. The Synod was very supportive. 5. Lay leadership was developed – people were trained."

[76] The invitation to the soon-to-be pastors was something like this: "We can't pay you much. You'll need to live in a troubled neighborhood. The parish has been in decline for years. You'll need to agree to stay for at least 7 years. We'll expect a lot of you and will stand with you in the process."

[77] Jonathan Aitken – "In 1974 he became a Conservative Member of Parliament spending eighteen years on the backbenches until being appointed Minister of State for Defense in 1992. He joined the Cabinet as Chief Secretary to the Treasury in 1994. His political career ended when he told a lie on oath in a libel action. Subsequently he pleaded guilty to charges of perjury and served a seven-month prison sentence in 1999.

After graduating with Distinction in theology after two years at Wycliffe Hall, Oxford (2000-2002) he began a new career as a writer, lecturer, and broadcaster." From Atken's web site. He attends St Matthew's, Westminster.

[78] In Deborah Soloman's inteview of Mike Huckabee, *The New York Times*, December 20, 2009.

[79] "We were losing the more traditional form of faith which saw religion as a practical activity. Like driving, swimming, dancing or gymnastics, you learn the truths of faith only by constant, dedicated practice - not by reading texts or adopting a metaphysical 'belief'. Like a myth, a religious doctrine is essentially a program of action. It makes no sense unless it is translated into practical action that helps you to dethrone egotism, selfishness and greed by practicing compassion to all living beings. In the book, I try to show how doctrines like the Incarnation or Trinity were originally a summons to selflessness and compassion and that we only discover their truth by making these qualities a reality in our own lives." Karen Armstrong, discussing her book "The Case for God" *Washington Post* web site, October 8, 2009.

[80] *After You Believe: Why Christian Character Matters*, N.T. Wright, Harper One, 2010. page 70.

[81] Ibid, page.17.

[82] Thomas Merton, *Life and Holiness*, Doubleday, 1963, pages. 118 – 119.

[83] Hymn 645; *The Hymnal 1982*.

[84] Diana Butler Bass, *Christianity for the Rest of Us*, page 280. Harper One, 2006.

[85] *Fill All Things,* page 125.

[86] Ibid, page 142.

[87] Ibid, page 156.

[88] Ibid, page 135